GARDEN
TO
SAVE THE
WORLD

GARDEN
TO
SAVE THE
WORLD

A feel-good guide
to growing for yourself,
your plants and the planet

Joe Clark

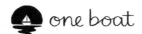

First published 2024 by One Boat
an imprint of Pan Macmillan
The Smithson, 6 Briset Street, London EC1M 5NR
EU representative: Macmillan Publishers Ireland Ltd, 1st Floor,
The Liffey Trust Centre, 117–126 Sheriff Street Upper,
Dublin 1, D01 YC43
Associated companies throughout the world
www.panmacmillan.com

ISBN 978-1-0350-3231-0

3 5 7 9 8 6 4 2

A CIP catalogue record for this book is available from the British Library.

Illustrations by Kamile Sakalauskaite

Printed and bound by CPI Group (UK) Ltd, Croydon, CR0 4YY

Visit **www.panmacmillan.com/bluebird** to read more about all our books
and to buy them. You will also find features, author interviews and
news of any author events, and you can sign up for e-newsletters
so that you're always first to hear about our new releases.

For my great-grandmother, Maisy

Contents

1

Welcome to my garden

The garden is my happy place. It has taught me so much, provided me with abundance, connected me with nature and, most importantly, brought me so much happiness. No matter what life has thrown my way, the garden has always helped me with the solution. Being outside in my garden brings me so much joy, and I know yours can do the same for you, too; the key is learning how to unlock its potential. This is my motivation for writing this book. I aim to help provide you with a few of those keys, and, hopefully, help you to connect with the outdoors in a way you may not have thought possible. Whether you have rolling acres of land, a window box, or anything in between, if you have been gardening for decades or are just starting out, I promise there will be something for everyone.

The end is nigh! Or is it?

I am not sure about you, but I would like a break from all the bad news. Especially bad news regarding the natural world, which at the moment seems to be constant. Doomsday is approaching and the end is nigh! Or at least that is what certain areas of the media seem to want us to believe right now. Sure, we are facing some challenges, but I am sorry to say that way of highlighting it simply does not help anyone. Instead of spreading negativity and mass panic, I would like to offer an alternative approach, by showing how what we do with our gardens can help. I truly believe our gardens hold the key to unlocking a brighter, more positive future, not just on an environmental level but a human level too. I aim to highlight how we can garden and use our gardens to help out, in a more positive and motivational manner. If by the end of the book you are feeling inspired to pop on your welly boots and get outside, then I have succeeded.

Our gardens may seem like little fragmented bits of land, but that is not how I think we should look at them. In the UK alone there are an estimated twenty-two million private gardens, which combined make up nearly four hundred and fifty thousand hectares, which is a tad over one million football pitches! And that is just the UK. Add in the USA, and the number of gardens jumps another seventy million. Collectively our gardens are so much more powerful than we could ever imagine.

When it comes to gardening, not only do I believe in bending the rules, I think it is essential to do so. As a result, please treat this book as a guide, not a set of definitive rules. Together, we are going to look at a range of ways we can use our gardens, including growing and storing your own food at home, upcycling, rewilding and even its health benefits, but please feel free to adapt any part of this book to suit your own style. You may be in another country, where there are different animals and plants, your seasons may fall at a different time of the year, or you may simply have slightly different goals. All of this is what makes gardening great! Remember, my ideas are just suggestions. Play around, test what works and does not work for you, and, most importantly, have fun!

So how did I get to this point?

Before we get started, I have to admit that I have never been to any form of horticultural college, I have not won any gold medals at prestigious gardening shows (although I did win the biggest pumpkin one year at a county fair), nor do I have a professional background in wildlife conservation. As a result, there will be no fancy jargon, Latin plant or animal names, or technical gardening principles, which in all honesty I do not think is a bad thing. There are plenty of books and encyclopaedias out there that cover this information anyway. I have read many of them, and have to admit, they are pretty heavy reading and the average casual gardener will get little benefit from them. What I do have, however, is more than twenty-five years of real-world practical experience of being outside in the garden, with possibly the best non-official gardening education, from the best teacher I could have ever asked for.

That teacher was my great-grandmother, who fortunately I lived next door to as a child. I owe so much to my great-grandmother; she showed me the ropes of gardening long before I even knew what was going on. I have pictures of her pushing me around the garden in my pram, where I could not have been any more than a few months old. As soon as I could walk, well, that was it. Every chance we had, we would be side by side, outside in the garden. The natural world fascinated me, and luckily, like a sponge, I absorbed as much information as I could from her.

She taught me everything, from my daffodils to my roses, and my carrots to my beetroot. The plants were important, but the education did not stop there! We spent just as much time looking at insects and wildlife as we did plants. I have countless happy memories of summers spent chasing butterflies, learning the difference between frogs

and toads and watching the different birds that would descend onto her bird table. She made sure I understood the importance this wildlife has in the garden, and how having a successful garden does not stop just at the plants.

Now when I think about it, she was way ahead of her time. She understood the importance of wildlife, and having a balanced garden. You have to remember, this was at a time when pesticides and plastics ruled the gardening world. At the age of eighty-five, she became the first person I knew who started recycling. This love of recycling also spilled into the garden, where we would look to see what we could repurpose. Milk bottles soon turned into watering cans, and lolly sticks into plant labels. Back then this was a bit strange, but today we know it as upcycling.

My great-grandmother showed me not only the joys of nature and the importance a balanced garden can have on your plants and local wildlife, but she left me with possibly an even greater gift: the gift of understanding how, if used right, our gardens can literally shape the world we live in!

It was not until I was in secondary school that I realized just how lucky I was. One day at lunchtime a red kite (which is a large bird of prey species found in the UK) swooped down into the playground. Everybody screamed. 'Eagle, eagle, look at the eagle' and ran all over the place. Not one person knew this was a red kite; not even one of the nearby teachers. This, for me, was the wakeup call I needed! After that day I decided to begin sharing some of the information my great-grandmother left me, so others could start to understand the joys of the natural world outside our back door.

I started to devour any gardening and nature books I could get my hands on, even heading to charity shops to see if I could find any old ones too, so I could understand the evolution of the garden over time.

I can say honestly that I have probably read most gardening books published in the UK during the last fifty years. I counted up all my gardening books the other day and I have at least two hundred! And this number does not include the ones I have given to other people over the years too.

This love of gardening literature was accelerated by my time at university. While I knew I had a love and passion for gardening, nature and helping others experience the benefits of both, I was unsure if I would be able to turn it into a career. So, I packed my bags and headed off to university, where I decided to read law. University helped me understand how to effectively research topics and then start to analyze what I had researched. All of a sudden, I was not just reading gardening books, I was analyzing them – not from a critical point of view, but rather from a more practical one, taking sections from each and experimenting in my own garden. This combined with the teachings from my great-grandmother helped me to mould my own style of gardening and allowed me to connect with nature in a way that was personal to me.

Three years flew by and before long it was time to graduate and go into the world of work. Naturally, after studying law, I decided to pursue a law career. However, I soon realized this was not my cup of tea. It was the only period of my life where I started to lose touch with nature and gardening, even missing an entire growing season, which is my favourite time of the year. This highlighted just how important that part of my life is to me. After only a month of two of being away from the garden and nature I found my mood slipping drastically, and I was surprised just how much I missed being outside. It was a hard decision to make, but I knew deep down I was pursuing the wrong career.

I left the world of law, and soon after I started working as a manager for the clothing company Abercrombie & Fitch. My four years there were great, and there was one area of management that I really enjoyed: training and educating team members. This gave me the confidence I needed to start sharing my gardening journey online, to hopefully start to educate others. My goal was to share some of the lessons my great-grandmother taught me, with some of my research over the years, combined with my love of helping to educate and train people, to help and inspire a few people online.

It took me three weeks to finally build up the confidence to post my first video. The video was uploaded in the morning, and then I went about my day hoping it might get ten views, but to my surprise later that evening when I checked, it had eight hundred views! In the previous ten years I had been able to help probably around eighty people experience the joys of gardening, and with the click of a button in a day I had reached ten times more people. From that moment I was hooked!

Fast forward to today, and the power of social media has allowed me to reach a far larger audience. I am lucky to share my garden with a 'growing' family of nearly two million people worldwide, with over four hundred million video views. By you picking up this book, I would like to welcome you to our growing family too!

What is a garden, and more importantly, what is a gardener?

I repeatedly refer to gardens, and us gardeners, throughout this book, so I think it is important I briefly explain what each term means to me.

A garden for me is any outside space, big or small, of which a gardener is the guardian, even if only for a short period of time, until it passes on to the next person to look after. It is easy to think gardening books are reserved only for those who have large sprawling gardens, but I want to showcase in this book how that is not true. You can achieve so much with just a few window boxes in a flat, or if you have a balcony, especially a sunny one, you will be surprised at how much you can do. Yes, with a smaller garden you may not be able to do everything you can do in a larger garden, but trust me, you will be able to accomplish more than you might think is possible.

Even if you do not have any form of garden at all, there are quite a few ways you can get involved. Some countries will offer you the chance to get an allotment. This is a patch of land, traditionally used to grow food, which you can rent, for a very modest fee, from your local council or even sometimes a charity or private land owner. If your country does not offer allotments, then look for shared or community gardens. While one of these may not be your own plot of land, you can still harness a lot of the benefits a garden would offer.

A common misconception may be that gardeners are usually people of a certain age, attending to their roses. While there is absolutely nothing wrong with this, especially as roses are one of my favourite flowers, that limited image is not really an accurate reflection of all I deem gardeners to be. In fact, just by you picking up this book, or even showing any interest in your garden or other outside space, in my eyes that makes you a gardener too!

I honestly do not believe there has been another time where gardening has been so cool and so popular. Head to your local garden centre and you will see what I mean. There will be a diverse mix of

people, all buying what they need to enjoy their gardens, and this fills me with joy. More and more people are starting to understand the benefit of this patch of ground outside our door, which we call a garden.

Okay, enough about me! Let's put on our gardening shoes and get outside. Please remember, you do not have to implement every part of this book to have a successful garden. Pick and choose what is relevant for your space, and trust me, you will have the garden of your dreams, bursting with life, making a positive impact for us all in no time! Finally, but most importantly, do not forget to have fun!

Your garden supermarket

Let's grow our own groceries!

I believe one of the best ways to harness the benefits of your garden, both individual and environmental, is by starting to grow your own food at home. Strong claim, I know! However, I have always thought there is something almost enchanting about the process. The way it connects you with nature, and allows you to understand just how perfectly balanced and magical the natural world is, just fascinates me. The process of planting a small seed and helping it on its journey to become a fully grown plant, which produces food, still captivates me after twenty-six years. The bountiful harvests that come as a result, are, for me, just a bonus.

However, I may be a little bit biased. My love of gardening and all things nature comes directly from my love of growing fruit and vegetables, as this was my gateway into the world of gardening, and one I am very glad I opened.

I was very lucky as a child, as this lifestyle of growing food at home was presented to me by both sets of grandparents. Due to this, I associate growing my own food at home with happy warm summer childhood memories.

Recently I came across the term 'core memory'. A core memory is usually one that is always there in your mind no matter how old you get. A memory so powerful, it is easy to picture it vividly, transporting you back in time. One common theme runs through nearly all of my core memories, which is that they are all outside in the garden. For this reason, I encourage anyone reading this who may have children or younger members of the family to get them involved too! You never know, chances are you will create a core memory or two.

Many people believe you need a large garden to successfully grow your own food at home. I am on a mission to dispel this way of thinking. Yes, if you would like to become completely self-sufficient you will need quite a large area to grow all that food. If I am being completely honest, very few people have the time to even think about that option. When I talk about growing your own food at home in this chapter, I am mainly talking about supplementing your food shops, not necessarily replacing them.

Growing food really is easy. I successfully did so as a child, using seeds from my rabbit's food. I do not say this to brag, but rather to give you the confidence to start. Harvesting a basket of freshly grown food from your garden really is one of the most satisfying feelings in the world. This, combined with the amazing taste, environmental benefits and money-saving possibilities, makes growing your own food one of the best ways to utilize your garden!

Why bother growing your own food?

One of the most common questions I am asked has to be, 'Why do you bother with all this work when we have supermarkets?' I completely understand this question, however, my response is always the same. Try not to view growing food at home as just a means to have food for your consumption. If you do, then unfortunately you may be missing the point. I like to think about it in the same way as listening to music. Sure, you can buy the CD (or more likely these days listen on your phone), but people go to concerts. Why is that? Usually it is because of the event itself, the atmosphere, the sound and all the extras that come with a live concert, not just for the music. Growing your own food is exactly the same: there are far more layers to the process than just the final product!

The number of people who are growing fruit and vegetables has boomed in recent years, which is absolutely amazing! There are many possible reasons, both individual and environmental, as to why this may have happened:

Eat fresh

I ran a poll on my Joe's Garden social media accounts, and of the fifteen thousand respondents, the overwhelming majority of people who grow their own food at home gave as their number one motivation for doing so the desire to have access to fresh produce. There is no getting away from the fact, homegrown food just tastes better. This is mainly due to the food being grown and harvested perfectly ripe while it is in season, and usually consumed soon after. Food straight from the garden really is a treat. The texture is still crispy, the fragrance fills your nose with joy and the sugars are yet to turn to starch, which gives some crops a truly sweet flavour. I am getting hungry just thinking about this!

Shop-bought produce simply cannot compete with these flavours.

There is often a long process from harvesting the food to getting it onto the supermarket shelves. This usually results in a below-par product, which often tastes bland at best. It is for this exact reason that I give so much homegrown food away to other people. The number of times I have heard comments like, 'Wow, lettuce isn't actually bland', or 'I never knew cucumbers actually have a taste'. That really is the beauty of homegrown produce.

I also believe one of the reasons homegrown food tastes so much better is because of the amount of time, love and effort that often goes into growing it. It is frequently said: the harder you work, the sweeter the reward; well, I think that is definitely true with homegrown food!

Engage with nature

Due to our busy modern lives, we are arguably less connected to nature than we have ever been. Before the Industrial Revolution, in the UK roughly 98 per cent of people earned their living through farming; today that number is around 0.4 per cent. As a result, we have lost that daily connection we once had with the natural world, and growing even just a little bit of food is a great way to reconnect.

I have found engaging with nature to be possibly the most beneficial activity I can do for my mental health. Growing my own food over the years has allowed me to connect with nature, on so many levels. If you do the same, you will start to become more aware about how entwined the natural world is, from the organic compost used to grow your plants, to the insects that help pollinate the flowers and the weather conditions needed for the overall success of everything.

It is really funny how your mindset changes once you start growing your own food. When I was very little, I used to think of bees as a pest, especially when they came to have a sniff of my summer picnics. However, from the age of around seven, I started to understand what beautiful and important little creatures they are. Bees are just one example of many that I could have chosen though.

Reduce air miles

In more developed nations such as the UK, we import fresh fruits and veg from all over the globe. Now I completely understand for some crops this is necessary. Bananas, mango and pineapple are all great examples of crops that are almost impossible to grow on a large scale in my UK climate. However, for some crops there is very little need for them to be shipped all across the globe, travelling thousands of miles, adding tonnes of carbon and other nasties to the atmosphere, when they can easily be grown locally.

Over the last year I have kept a record of where each of the main supermarkets have sourced their fresh produce from. Now please bear in mind, I looked at each vegetable when it was in season in the UK. I even waited until I was harvesting that exact fruit or vegetable in my garden or allotment, before seeing where the same crop being sold in the supermarket had come from.

While there were a few British-grown crops, each and every one of these British crops had an imported option alongside it. Something I will never understand is that the limited British options were also on the whole more expensive too! How is it possible that food grown in countries such as New Zealand – then picked, packaged and flown around the globe – is cheaper than the same food grown on a farm an hour up the road from where I live?

Opposite is a table containing all the crops I grew over the last year, and where my local supermarkets selling those same crops at the same time of the year got theirs from.

As you can see, the vast majority of crops have sometimes need-lessly travelled thousands of miles to end up on our shelves. I say

Type of Produce	Where was it grown?	Approx. miles from UK*
Apples	NZ / South Africa	116,00 / 5,600
Apricots	Spain	787
Asparagus	Mexico	5,500
Baby corn	Kenya	4,230
Baby cucumbers	Spain	787
Baby tomatoes	Morocco	1,300
Basil	Italy	900
Beetroot	Spain	787
Blueberries	Turkey	1760
Brussels sprouts	Morocco	1300
Butternut squash	Namibia	5200
Cantaloupe melons	Spain	787
Carrots	Italy	900
Chard	Netherlands	221
Chillies	Senegal	2700
Cucumbers (also baby)	Spain	787
Fennel	Italy	900
Garlic	France	220
Grapes	Egypt	2,180
Green beans	Morocco	1,300
Kiwi	Chile	7,250
Leeks	Spain	787
Lemongrass	Kenya	4230
Lemons	South Africa	5600
Limes	Brazil	5400
Mangetout	Peru	6300
Mushrooms	Poland	900

* Approx. miles as the crow flies, from capital city to capital city.

Type of produce	Where was it grown?	Approx. miles from UK*
Onions (red)	Spain	787
Onions (white)	Chile	7,250
Oranges	Peru	5,400
Passion fruit	Colombia	5,300
Peaches	Spain	787
Pears	Netherlands	221
Peas	Spain	787
Peppers	Italy	900
Plums	Spain	787
Raspberries	Spain	787
Rocket	Italy	900
Rosemary	Italy	900
Spring onions	Senegal	2700
Strawberries	Egypt	2180
Sweet potatoes	Portugal	980
Sweetcorn	Spain	787
Tarragon	Germany	578
Thyme	Kenya	4,230
Tomatoes (also baby)	Morocco	1,300

* Approx. miles as the crow flies, from capital city to capital city.

sometimes, because occasionally crops can fail. This is usually due to adverse weather or disease, and when this occurs there is no option but to fly some produce in from other areas of the globe.

The miles this food has travelled is only part of the problem. Many of the countries on this list are hot and often dry. Growing fruit and vegetables frequently requires a lot of water and other precious resources. An example of why this could become more of an issue is that many of these countries are experiencing increased droughts.

Morocco, for example, appears three times on this list, and over the last two decades the level and intensity of droughts in the country has dramatically increased; 2022 saw its worst drought in forty years! If this trend continues it could force us to rethink where our fresh produce is coming from in the not-too-distant future.

Reduce dependency on supermarkets

Our usual abundance of fresh food has been challenged in a lot of ways lately. It has really highlighted for me why being completely reliant on supermarkets might not be a good idea! Empty shelves where fresh produce was once in good supply are now all too common. If you are lucky enough to find full shelves, the price increases are enough to put you off buying anyway!

When you grow your own food, it is actually pretty common to end up growing too much. It is very hard to grow a mixture of different crops all maturing at different times to give you a perfect balance of food. What often happens is you grow an abundance of one or two crops, which are all ready to eat at the same time, leaving you with too much food. I end up with a glut (usually of tomatoes) every single year, and every year I donate some to local food charities. They are always grateful, but this year I have noticed they were even more so. I assume this is in part due to these shortages, price increases and the cost of living crisis.

Growing your own food also gives you far more control. You know exactly what variety it is, where it has come from and whether any pesticides or other chemicals have been used during the growing process. You can also grow varieties and crops you may not often see in the supermarkets. A great example of a crop that is so much fun to grow at home is cucamelons. You might be thinking, what are those? And that is my point exactly. They are super easy to grow at home, the seeds are widely available, but you will be hard pressed to find them in the supermarkets. Growing food at home really does provide you with such a wide range of weird and wonderful fruits and veggies.

Help to reduce your waste

Growing your own food at home helps to cut out a lot of waste in many different ways, the most obvious one being the sheer volume of packaging you will save. If you have a close look at the fresh produce in the supermarkets, one thing that will really stand out is the volume of packaging used to wrap it. It is everywhere and often plastic! By growing your own food, you eliminate quite a bit of this packaging, and throughout the year this will really start to add up.

With homegrown food you have the option to harvest your crops as and when you need them, or once they are perfectly ripe. This not only increases the flavour, as we mentioned earlier, but it also dramatically reduces food waste, as you are only harvesting what you need, when you need it.

Growing your own food will often encourage you to start upcycling and composting, both of which will help reduce the amount of waste that would otherwise most likely find its way into landfill. These are both topics we will explore at length in chapter five (see page 126).

Have fun with friends, family or even yourself

The main reason I grow food at home is that it is fun. I enjoy knowing I am helping the environment, and I also enjoy eating fresh fruit and veggies. However, the part I enjoy the most is the process of growing the food.

I believe the key to having fun when growing your own food is not to put too much pressure on yourself. Accept that something is going to go wrong; heck, in my garden things go wrong all the time! Get creative, try different foods, build different upcycling projects and just try your best! I promise you the satisfaction of strolling out into the garden and harvesting a basket of fresh food is worth every penny spent and every bit of hard work you have put into growing it!

I often garden alone, which if I am being honest I quite enjoy. However, from time to time it is really fun getting friends and family involved too, especially for those larger projects, where at the end you can reward them with a treat or two from the garden.

Top tip

If you want to get children involved in gardening, you need to keep it fun. The best way I have found to do this is to plant crops that are fast growers, as children need to see results straight away. I highly recommend growing crops such as radishes or salad leaves, as they can be ready to harvest in as little as thirty days! Getting children to connect with nature is one of the best ways we can help protect the environment for years to come, as they are more likely to show empathy towards environmental issues if they have a good connection to the environment. Growing food is a great way to introduce them to the natural world, and I always find earthworms are a big hit with children too!

What do you need to get started?

I hope by now you are itching to at least give growing your own food a go. After all, there really is very little to lose and a lot to gain. Before we get stuck into the details of how to go about it, it is probably a good idea to have a little chat about what tools and equipment you might need. The great part about growing your own food, and gardening in general, is you can spend as much or as little money as you want to.

Until recently I spent practically no money on my garden. Not because I didn't want to, but because I was a student with no money to spend. I am now lucky enough to have a pretty high-tech vegetable garden, with various raised beds and irrigation systems. Does this make my life easier? Yes. Are my harvests any better? No, not really! That is the best part about growing your own food at home. A tomato does not care if it is being grown in a £20,000 greenhouse or a £75 polytunnel. A pepper does not care if it is being watered with an old upcycled milk bottle, or a £300 irrigation system. Ultimately, if you look after your plants, they will look after you. Yes, fancy tools and gadgets will make this easier, but I went twenty-two years without them, and if I had more time to look after my plants like I used to, I would probably still not have any fancy gadgets.

My simple take-away point here is to dip your toe in first. Start with a few basic bits of equipment, and then once the gardening bug has bitten, which it will, you can begin to add more and more.

In chapter five of this book, we explore the wonderful world of up-cycling (see page 126). There are so many amazing ways you can upcycle old bits of waste into practically everything you need for your garden. Not only does this save you a fortune, but it helps prevent that potential waste from entering landfill.

Equipment I recommend

It is almost impossible to give you a list of equipment you must have in your garden. Honestly, it depends on so many different factors, such as what you are trying to grow and where you live. If you live in Arizona, for example, a greenhouse is the last thing I would put on your list. Whereas if you live in Scotland, it would be one of the first!

You will also need to think about what type of growing you will be doing. If you are growing in containers, then really all you need are the containers themselves, compost, seeds and water. If you are growing in open ground, however, I would recommend you get a little more equipment.

So here is my list of equipment I would recommend you consider getting, if you wish to start growing your own food at home. Anything marked with a (U) can be easily made by upcycling, and we explore many of these in chapter five. Please do not take this list as gospel, it is simply equipment that I use in my own garden and would highly recommend. You will not necessarily need everything on this list, just pick and choose what you think will be required for your needs. If you are growing in containers then obviously you will not need a shovel, for example.

I recommend:

* A good pair of gloves
* Secateurs or plant snips
* Hand trowel
* Plant labels (U)
* Two watering cans – one small and one large, both with rose attachments (U)
* Water butt to collect rainwater (U)
* Seed dibber (U)
* Pencil
* Twine

* Bamboo canes
* Bamboo cane eye protectors (U)
* Frost fleece or bubble wrap
* Airtight/secure container to store your seeds
* Shovel (for scooping and moving earth, sand, manure, etc.)
* Spade (for digging)
* Garden fork
* A range of pots and containers (U)
* Some form of plant protection, whether it is a polytunnel, cold frame or greenhouse (U)
* Scissors
* Spray bottle
* Garden shoes you do not mind getting dirty
* Hoe
* Kneeling pad (trust me, once you try one you will never be without one)
* Basic first aid kit
* A minimum/maximum thermometer

Just a reminder, you do not *need* any of this. But it will make your life a lot easier if you have some of it.

Top tip

Do not buy everything at once as this will often lead you to buy items quite cheap. Instead, buy less, but buy higher quality. With a little bit of care, good-quality garden equipment can last a long time and is well worth the investment. Remember to also utilize second-hand shops and online communities as well as local swaps.

Power tools or hand tools?

When it comes to garden tools and equipment, you will often have the choice of power tools or hand-held tools. Power tools have exploded in popularity over the last few years and the range you can buy is currently growing rapidly. Head to any garden or DIY shop and there will be an extensive display, almost like some sort of *Men in Black* wall of weapons.

I am not denying power tools have a place in the garden. They do. Especially in larger gardens. And power tools might also be essential for people with certain mobility issues. However, I suggest they may have become a bit too common. If you do not believe me, head to any suburb on a warm, summer weekend and just listen. You'll hear a chorus of lawn mowers, strimmers, hedge trimmers and pretty much every other type of power tool you can think of. Where I live, it is all I hear from dawn to dusk during the summer months, with the main culprit being lawn mowers.

The noise pollution is annoying, but it is the *actual* pollution from these tools that is more of a problem. Many power tools use petrol to generate their power. Now obviously if you have a massive garden with giant lawns, a petrol-powered lawn mower is really your only option. However, the vast majority of people, including myself and my neighbours, have more modest spaces, where these petrol power tools are completely overkill. Instead, I would suggest having a look at some of the hand tool alternatives.

In smaller gardens these are far more effective: often just as fast, help to keep you active, are more neighbourly and miles better for the environment. Power tools tend to cause harm to the environment, whereas hand tools help you to better connect with it.

Now please do not think I am on a protest here to ban power tools. I am not, and never will, as some people rely on them. I would just like to maybe offer a few alternatives to think about:

Power tool	Hand tool alternative
Chainsaw	Bowsaw
Lawn mower	Push reel mower
Hedge trimmer	Hand shears
Strimmer	Long-handle shears
Sprinkler	Watering can
Rotavator	Garden fork
Leaf blower	Broom
Jet washer	Wire brush

Other than the reduction in noise and the benefit to the environment, hand tools will save you a considerable amount of money too. Hand tools will usually be far cheaper to purchase, cheaper to use and less expensive to maintain. So maybe next time you are thinking about buying a power tool, have a little look at the hand equivalent and weigh up what one is best for you.

Top tip

When buying power tools, it is often a good idea to consider electric or battery powered over petrol. Electric in most cases will be better for the environment, far less noisy and just all round better suited to casual garden use. Just be careful around the wires, as sharp blades and electrical wires are not a great combination.

Gardening clothes

Avoid buying new clothes specially for use in the garden, and instead try to repurpose old ones. Trust me, when you are outside growing your own food, your clothes are going to get damaged. If I am out gardening in my nice clothes and shoes, rather than getting lost in the gardening and reaping all the benefits that come with it, I am more concerned about damaging my clothes. So, I like to wear old clothes, where is it no big deal if they get stained or ripped, because it will happen at some point.

I have four categories of clothes in my wardrobe. What I call my high-quality going-out clothes, my everyday clothes, lounging around clothes and garden clothes. Unlike all the others, garden clothes are not bought for their purpose. Instead, they are often old versions of clothes from each category. You will often find me out in the garden wearing an old shirt paired with a pair of sports shorts. Who cares what it looks like? As long as it is functional, it is going to end up in my gardening wardrobe.

If you do want to buy some clothes to use in the garden, then I highly recommend having a look in charity shops. These clothes will be cheaper, and buying from charity shops can help slow the amount of clothing that ends up being thrown away. Clothing waste and fast fashion has become a massive environmental threat, and us garden-ers do not need to be making it worse. Instead, view your gardening wardrobe as a brilliant way to utilize old clothes.

However, the one item I would advise you go out and buy is a good pair of garden shoes. Welly boots immediately spring to mind for the UK, but I actually prefer a pair of proper boots. They offer plenty of support without going half way up my leg. I mean, after all, we are growing a bit of fresh food, not running a full-scale farm. If you are container gardening, a good pair of shoes is less important than if you are digging a large vegetable patch in the ground.

Be realistic about space

When you set out to grow your own food at home it is important to work *with* the space you have, not against it. Many people assume growing food at home is reserved for those with only the biggest gardens. Once upon a time that may have been true, but gardening has changed so much over the last fifty years. Today, having a small space is not a reason to abandon your ambition to grow some food at home. In fact, I would say having a small space is not a bad thing at all. I recommend everyone starts off small, regardless of how much room you have.

If you are just starting out, I think it is important to remind yourself that the goal is to not necessarily replace the supermarkets, but rather to supplement your food shops, have a little fun, and learn a new skill or two. So, let's explore the main ways you can grow your own fruit and veg at home, and identify what method might be the best option for you and your available space.

When it comes to growing fruit and veg at home there are really three main ways you can do this. You can grow in the traditional way of planting directly into the soil, otherwise known as open ground gardening; you can use pots and containers; or you can grow in raised beds, which is sort of a crossover between the two.

Growing food in containers

For all beginners, regardless of how much space you have, I recommend starting out by using containers. This is possibly the easiest way to grow food, and they will fit into pretty much any size space. I have friends who have turned their balconies into thriving urban gardens by using just a few containers.

Containers come in all different shapes, sizes and materials. In chapter five (see page 138), we explore this in some detail and discuss the pros and cons of each material.

Even though I am lucky enough to have quite a large garden, I still grow quite a few crops in containers. This is because there are so many pros of container growing, including:

* Pots are perfect for small spaces as you can select the size you need for your space.

* There are now more eco-friendly alternatives to plastic, such as bamboo and natural-fibre pots.

* You have the added benefit of being able to move your plants around. This is amazing as you can bring plants inside if it is cold, move them into the shade if it is too hot or simply just change the look and feel of your space, without having to uproot and potentially damage any plants.

* A lot of people live in rented accommodation. Using pots and containers is perfect for renters, as it allows you to grow your own food without changing the property permanently. If you move out you can simply take all your containers with you.

* It is by far the cheapest way to get started. Growing food in containers does not require many tools. All you need is a good container, a high-quality compost, some seeds and a means of watering your containers.

* Containers allow you to control the soil you are using. It can be hard to change the soil structure in open ground, often taking years of work, but in pots and containers you can select the exact soil for your needs.

* You will not have to worry as much about weeds (unless you mix in soil from the garden).

* Crops in pots are much easier to protect from insects, slugs and hungry birds.

However, it is not all sunshine and rainbows. Growing in pots and containers does have its fair share of cons, including:

* Crops grown in pots will need to be watered more regularly, leading to a higher water usage to achieve a good harvest.

* You will often need to feed the soil in your containers far more than you might have to in open ground.

* Some crops simply cannot be grown effectively in pots. A great example is corn, one of my favourites to grow at home. Corn needs to be planted in large blocks as it is wind pollinated. If you plant one or two corn plants in containers, prepare to be disappointed.

* Many pots are made out of plastic, which, as we all know by now, is something we need to try to avoid. Throughout this book we will look at many various ways you can avoid these plastic pots, but the lure of cheap plastic containers will always be there for every container grower.

* Plants grown in containers can be quite hard to support. Often the pot is not deep enough to poke a cane into, and when it is, it can make the pot top heavy and vulnerable in the wind.

Overall, pots are fantastic for beginners and people with very small spaces who would like to try to grow a little bit of food at home.

> **Top tip**
> *When growing plants in containers it is essential these have drainage holes in the bottom. Without drainage, your soil will easily become waterlogged, which will more often than not lead to root rot killing your plant. Some pots will have the drainage holes, but be aware that you may need to poke out the holes yourself. I would also recommend that you avoid buying decorative pots that do not have drainage holes, as these are probably the easiest way to kill your plants. It is also a good idea to use a saucer underneath your pot to capture any water drainage, which you can then use to water your other plants.*

Growing food in open soil

If you are lucky enough to have a large garden, then growing your own food directly in the ground could be the best option for you. Even more so if you have lovely, rich, free-draining soil. A large garden will definitely help, but it is not essential. I have squeezed vegetable patches into all sorts of strange places in the past, almost in the same way you would with a flower border! Traditionally, nearly all food was grown in the ground, and there is no doubt this tried-and-tested method will certainly work.

I would just like to add, growing food in the ground can require quite a bit of work to get it prepared. If you know growing your own food is something you would love to do, then go for it. However, if you just want to try to give growing your own food at home a go to see if you enjoy it, this is probably not the best way to go about it.

Please remember, when you are making your vegetable patch you cannot easily move it like you can with containers and raised beds. Spend a bit of time planning where you would like it to be, thinking of factors such as how much sunlight each area gets, is it going to be in the way of anything, is it easily accessible and does it suit your garden design. Remember, your vegetable patch can be any shape or size you would like. I mean, I have got all sorts of different shapes in my garden, and for me it adds a bit of character, and gives it a more natural feel than rows of square or rectangular beds.

There are so many pros of growing your own food in open ground, a few of which include:

* You will be able to grow pretty much any crop, as you will often have more space.

* Growing crops in the ground will use far less water than growing in pots.

* Plants will often develop stronger, deeper root systems.

* It is far easier to support your plants in open ground as you can push canes and supports deep into the soil.

* Using the land you own comes with no immediate extra costs (however, you will need more tools to maintain/make a vegetable bed).

* Plants grown in the open soil will utilize rainwater better.

However, just like pots, growing in open soil does have some cons, including:

* Weeds, weeds and more weeds! There is no escaping weeds when you grow in open soil. There are ways to manage and

reduce weeds, but I am yet to find a way to eliminate them completely.

* Often your soil will need improving, with lots of organic matter, which can get expensive.

* You cannot easily move a vegetable garden. You have to fill it back in and start the whole process again.

* It is harder to protect your crops out in the open soil.

I would recommend growing your crops in open soil, but maybe not if you are a beginner. Learn the ropes using pots and raised beds, and once you have the bug, add in a few in-the-ground beds. I find my best crops come from my open-ground vegetable patch, but also it is worth adding that the most failures also come from my open vegetable patch.

> **Top tip**
> *I would highly advise, no matter what shape or size vegetable patch you create, to always incorporate walkways. This will help to avoid walking on the soil and compacting it, and just makes life a lot easier if everything is within reach.*

Growing food in raised beds

Raised beds are probably my favourite way to grow food at home. They are so versatile and come in all different shapes, sizes and materials. Some raised beds are just layers of compost over the top of garden soil, some are deep containers with open bottoms, others come with a bottom, and some raised beds are elevated in the air by legs.

In my garden I have nearly every type of raised bed, and they are all fantastic. If you want to start gardening but have mobility issues, or use a wheelchair, then raised beds are probably the best option for you.

These days you can buy a raised bed to fit any size garden, making them the perfect option for spaces from balconies through to large country gardens. It is worth noting raised beds can get quite expensive. However, I have only bought three of my eleven raised beds. Instead, I used old pallet wood to make my own, and trust me I have

The wonderful world of Hügelkultur

You are probably thinking, what on earth is that! Hügelkultur has been used for hundreds of years throughout parts of Europe. It is essentially the process of layering logs and plant debris to make a raised garden bed.

All of the raised beds in my garden utilize this method, and honestly it will save you a fortune on compost.

To get your hügelkultur beds started, place some larger logs along the base of your raised beds. Once you have your layer of larger logs, add smaller twigs, branches and bits of wood.

Now that your base of logs and twigs is in place, it is time to add in a layer of organic plant matter. I like to use old hay or straw, lawn trimmings and fallen autumn leaves. Over time this will all organically rot down, enriching the soil.

On top of my organic plant matter, I like to add a layer of homemade compost, that is at least 23 cm (9 inches) deep, to allow the roots of your plants to have plenty of room to grow. Some like to add a layer of topsoil to the compost, but I never do, as I do not think it adds much value and would rather save the money.

Some people will advise that you leave this material over the winter to rot down, but I have planted my raised beds the same day as building them.

zero carpentry skills, so if I can do it, you certainly can too. If you are interested in how I do this, you can find more information in chapter five (see page 141).

Just like pots and open soil, raised beds have so many benefits, and here are a few of my favourites:

* Raised beds can be easily made for free, using old pallet wood.

* They give you a balance between growing in pots and growing in open soil.

* If you avoid using garden soil to fill them up, you should not have a problem with weeds.

* Raised beds can often look very neat and attractive in the garden.

* More often than not they are made from wood or metal, which helps to avoid plastic usage.

* You can grow almost anything in raised beds; I successfully grow crops such as corn every year in my larger ones.

* Raised beds are fantastic for people with mobility issues, especially wheelchair users, or those less able to spend prolonged amounts of time bending down.

* While maybe not as portable as garden pots, raised beds can be relocated around the garden, or even to another property.

* As raised beds are slightly elevated off the floor, they will offer a little bit of ground frost protection.

* The soil in raised beds often warms up faster in the spring, allowing you to sow your crops a little bit earlier.

As you have probably guessed by now, raised beds do have some cons, and these include:

* If you cannot build your own raised beds, they can be quite expensive.

* Raised beds will need a lot of compost and high-quality soil. My larger raised beds have a 2,000-litre capacity (2.6 tonnes), which is fine if like me you have a lot of home-made compost, but if you are relying on store-bought, this will cost a fortune to fill.

* Slugs! A word that often sends shivers down gardeners' spines. Raised beds often give slugs the perfect place to live, as they settle between the compost and the inside wall of the raised bed.

* Plants growing in raised beds will still require quite a bit more water than plants growing in open soil.

Raised beds are undoubtedly fantastic, and I would be lost without mine! However, my advice for beginners would still be to start off growing in pots. Then once you have the bug for growing your own food, maybe invest in a raised bed (or make your own). If you are already growing crops at home in pots or in the soil, then for you, I cannot recommend raised beds enough.

Growing your own food at home 101

While this is not necessarily an out and out book on how to grow your own food, I cannot dangle the carrot in front of you, lure you in and then change topics. That would be cruel. So, let's go on a super quick crash course on how to grow your own food at home.

This is quite an extensive subject, so I can only scratch the surface here. I am a big advocate of experimenting in the garden. The advice below works well for me, but if you want to adapt it to your own technique, then I am all for that! Following the rules of gardening gets boring, so use this as a loose guide, and once you have a bit of success, add in your own touches to try to make things better.

Plants want to grow

I once heard the British gardener Alan Titchmarsh say something to the effect of: plants want to grow; it is down to us to stay out of the way. That observation really resonated with me. The seeds we grow really do want to grow, and often we overcomplicate the process, which actually puts the plants under more stress. Every year plants pop up across the garden that have self-seeded. I have had radishes grow in gravel paths, strawberry plants grow in the cracks in paving slabs and sunflowers grow out of a gutter! These are testament to a plant's will to grow, and it highlights the need for us to just let them do their thing. Sure, check in on them every now and again to make sure they are well watered and looking healthy, but for the most part leave them to grow; they will do most of the hard work for you.

The four essentials for plant success

I believe there are only four things your plants really need to successfully grow. These are: **sunlight**, **warmth**, **water** and **food**. There are other factors you can consider, but I believe in keeping it as simple as possible. If your plants are getting plenty of sunlight, are planted at the right time of the year, the roots are moist and growing in a nutrient-rich soil, then I promise you, your plants will be a success. It really is that simple.

Seed or plug plants?

You will often see little plug plants at the store. They are usually little seedlings, no bigger than a few centimetres (an inch or so), in small containers. Buying plug plants is a great way to start as it skips out the seed sowing, and worrying about germination. However, for me that is part of the fun. I recommend that if you have the space, try to start from seed. Not only will this save you a fortune, but it will reduce a lot of waste, as plug plants often come in little plastic strips, with plastic labels. Also, seeing your seedlings break through the soil to say hello is one of the most satisfying parts of growing your own food. Some of your seeds will most likely fail for various reasons, and this is where plug plants are really useful as a replacement.

Plant protection

Your plants are vulnerable to attack from a range of things, from insects and slugs to birds and deer, and even from extreme weather. It is important to keep an eye out for any signs of damage so you can address the issue. I prevent the vast majority of insect and animal damage by offering them alternatives to my crops. The birds have birdfeeders, the deer have sacrificial bushes I have planted just for them and the insects have wildlife borders that keep them happy. This is not always a hundred per cent effective, so I would also invest in some natural-fibre nets to help keep your crops from being eaten.

The weather at the moment seems to be causing more damage than animals or insects. Make sure your plants are protected to the best of your ability from any weather extremes, such as wind, heat or cold.

Give your plants room to grow

I understand how tempting it can be to ignore the spacing guidelines on your packet of seeds, to try to grow as much as possible. It might seem like a good idea, but trust me, you are far better off giving each plant plenty of room to grow. When you grow your plants too close together, each plant ends up competing with its neighbour. They compete for light, they compete for nutrients and they compete for moisture. Usually what happens is you end up with much weaker, smaller plants, which will produce a far lower yield of crops than one healthier plant would.

It is also really important to let air flow through and around your plants. If they are too close together not only will they struggle to grow, but they are more prone to disease, as there will be a severe reduction in airflow. Good airflow can not only help to carry away any spores, but also help prevent mould from forming due to the moisture plants naturally release.

Accept failure, but keep notes

All gardeners fail. I fail with at least one crop every single year, and often it's more than one. It is important you start you growing journey with this knowledge in the back of your mind. Otherwise, it can be easy to get demoralized, which is probably the main reason why people give up on growing their own food at home. The most important part of garden failures is to keep notes. Note down everything: what worked, what did not, when did you sow, what did you sow. Note this all down and it will help you identify what may have gone wrong and will help you prevent it from happening next year. An example in my garden is my runner beans. I had failed every single year. By looking at my notes I noticed I changed pretty much everything, other than the time of the year I sowed the seeds. So, the next year I changed that too, and just like magic they grew. It turned out I was sowing them too early.

When to water?

This has to be the most common question I get asked. Unfortunately, there is no magic answer. Different plants have different needs. Carrots are pretty drought resistant, for example, whereas tomatoes can really struggle without consistent watering. My advice for the vast majority of plants is to give them a really big drink, and just as the soil is starting to become dry again, give them another drink. I aim to keep the soil moist at all times, while also making sure the soil is not saturated. It is also important to try to avoid the plant itself when watering, and instead aim for the nearby soil.

When to harvest?

This comes down to personal preference, but I do have a few recommendations. It can be really tempting to let your produce grow as big as possible. While this can be fun, unless you are entering it in a local competition, it is not the best idea. When crops get really large, they often lose flavour, and the texture becomes tough. For the vast majority of crops, it is best to harvest them as soon as they are ripe. This is when I find there is the perfect balance of flavour and texture. It is also worth mentioning that the longer you wait to harvest, the higher the risk of damage to your crops. This could be due to insects, animals, weather or disease. Trust me, don't risk waiting too long to harvest, because the slugs and birds will more often than not beat you to it!

What to grow?

Having touched on some of the reasons, both personal and environmental, as to *why* growing your own food is a good idea, let's have a quick look at *what* you can grow.

My advice to anyone starting out is to grow what you enjoy eating. This might sound obvious, but it is all too tempting to try to grow all sorts of weird and wonderful crops. Stick to what you know you like to start off with. There will be plenty of time to experiment in the future.

I like to grow crops that follow this simple formula: if it is easy to grow, but expensive to buy or even hard to find in shops, then it goes to the top of my grow list. If a crop is hard to grow, but widely available in the shops, then it will be lower down on my grow list.

Here are a few examples of crops that are very easy to grow in my climate, which are often expensive, or not widely available in the shops:

* Kohlrabi
* Cape gooseberry
* Loofah
* Strawberries
* Blueberries
* Swiss chard
* Endive
* Asparagus
* Asparagus peas
* Cucamelon
* Fresh sweetcorn
* Salad leaves

When considering what crops to grow, possibly the most important factor is the variety. Take tomatoes, for example. I have grown over seventy varieties and there are still hundreds more to try. Have a little think about what you are after. Do you want big, small, sweet, colourful, indoors, outdoors, disease resistant, unusual or pretty much anything else you can think of? Picking the correct variety of a fruit or vegetable is the key to success, especially if you are growing in containers. If you are unsure as to what variety is best for your needs, and your climate, head to your local garden centre or plant nursery. They will be happy to have a chat with you, and help you select the best seeds or plug plants for your needs.

Let's talk about heirloom seeds

I cannot talk about seeds without briefly mentioning heirloom varieties. Heirloom seeds are, essentially, very old seed varieties. They are usually known for having distinct characteristics, from unusual colours to fantastic flavours. I love growing heirloom seeds, as I think there is something great in knowing you are growing the exact same variety that other people have been growing for hundreds of years.

Heirloom seeds, however, run the risk of becoming extinct. Modern seed varieties are replacing more and more heirloom varieties each year. Luckily, there are a few companies who are dedicated to saving these fantastic seeds, and here are a few reasons why you should think about choosing them:

* Heirloom seeds will save you money and reduce packaging waste. Heirloom seeds are open pollinated. This means if you grow a cucumber, for example, the seeds inside the cucumber you have grown will produce the same cucumber next year. A lot of modern seeds are hybrids, which means the seeds inside any resulting harvests are not guaranteed to produce the same variety when replanted. By saving seeds each year, you can save a lot of money, as well as save a lot of packaging too.

* Heirloom seeds are not genetically modified, helping to maintain the natural balance. You may hear this being referred to as 'non-GMO'.

* They have survived the test of time. Heirloom seeds are very reliable, as gardeners have, for many generations, selected and kept only the strongest and best varieties. This usually results in a very high-quality and delicious crop, with low wastage.

* Many heirloom seeds are organic, which refers to the process of how they are grown. Organic seeds have to meet with the organic regulations of each country where they are grown, which often have very strict rules on pest control and spraying crops with nasty chemicals, due to the impact they can have on local wildlife and the environment as a whole. However, while many are organic, some are not, so please check before buying if this matters to you, as this will change from seller to seller.

* I think there is something really exciting about growing and eating the same crops our great, great grandparents were eating. Plus, it is nice knowing you are helping to prevent these ancient seeds from becoming extinct.

Work with your weather, not against it

No matter what I do, I have to accept I am limited by the British weather. Wherever you live, you will have to respect your climate. Sure, you can use greenhouses and polytunnels to help, but if you try to fight the weather, you will lose every single time.

Without the help of artificial heat and light, I cannot grow certain crops, such as pineapples, so I do not waste my energy trying to do so. Instead, focus on what you can grow, there will be plenty of options for most climates.

Crops worth growing

As mentioned before, this is a highly individualistic topic; what one person may like, another may hate. I recommend you do your own research, and experiment with different crops, until you find what you like.

Having said that, I would like to offer a few recommendations of my favourite crops, as well as different crops for different conditions.

MY RECOMMENDATIONS FOR FAST-GROWING CROPS:

* Baby beetroot
* Broccoli raab
* Carrots
* Leafy greens
* Peas
* Micro greens
* Spinach
* Spring onions
* Sprouting seeds
* Summer radish (can grow in as little as 30 days!)
* Summer squash (like courgette/zucchini)

FUN FRUITS TO TRY TO GROW:

* Alpine strawberries
* Cape gooseberry
* Golden kiwi
* Gooseberry
* Logan berries
* Pink berries (the pink version of a blueberry)
* White berry (the white version of a blackberry)
* Wine grapes

CROPS TO TRY IN A SHADED SPOT:†

* Beetroot
* Carrots
* Kale
* Mibuna

† While these crops will grow in shaded spots, they will always grow better with some direct sunlight.

‡ Top tip – please grow your mint in pots or containers as it can easily spread across open ground

* Mint‡
* Mizuna
* Pea shoots

* Radish
* Spinach
* Swiss chard

MY FAVOURITE CROPS TO GROW IN A SMALL SPACE:

* Bush tomatoes
* Cape gooseberries
* Carrots
* Cucumbers
* Dwarf beans
* Dwarf peas

* Herbs
* Lettuce leaves
* Peppers/chillies
* Radishes
* Spring onions
* Strawberries

MY TOP PICKS FOR BEGINNERS:

* Beetroot
* Grapes
* Lettuce
* Peas
* Peppers
* Potatoes
* Pumpkins

* Radishes
* Raspberries
* Runner beans
* Strawberries
* Swiss chard
* Tomatoes

My Dos and Don'ts of Growing Food at Home

✓ Wait until the soil has warmed up, before planting outside. A general indicator that your soil is getting warmer is when little weeds start to appear!

✓ Grow your plants in a sunny spot in the garden

✓ If growing in containers, make sure they have drainage holes

✓ Water young plants regularly

✓ Enrich your soil by adding in lots of organic matter

✓ Feed your plants with a good liquid feed, especially once they start to crop

✓ Label your seed sowings and plants, to prevent them getting mixed up

✓ Give your plants plenty of room to grow

✓ Harvest regularly, as this will prompt some crops to produce more

✓ Stagger seed sowings to allow for multiple harvests

✓ Encourage wildlife such as frogs and hedgehogs into your vegetable patch, as they will act as a natural 'pest' control

✓ Try to water your plants as consistently as possible, and avoid letting your soil completely dry out

✓ Water in the mornings or evenings, to prevent evaporation when the sun is at its warmest in the middle of the day

✓ Keep seed packets as they contain valuable information on growing your crops

- ✘ Plant your crops in full shade

- ✘ Grow large varieties in small containers

- ✘ Try to grow crops that are not suited for your climate

- ✘ Sow all of your seeds at once, this will often lead to a glut of food all in one go

- ✘ Plant too much, as this can soon become overwhelming

- ✘ Use peat-based composts

- ✘ Water during the heat of the day, as this can scorch the leaves, and cause a lot of evaporation

- ✘ Leave store-bought plants in the small pots they come in from the shops

- ✘ Plant in containers that have no drainage holes

- ✘ Trample the dug soil after planting

- ✘ Over-fertilize with manure

- ✘ Try to plant your crops out of season

- ✘ Let weeds grow in your vegetable patch

- ✘ Use very old seeds, as the germination rate will be much lower

- ✘ Put too much pressure on yourself

Now that you have some guidelines under your belt, create a list of everything you need to start growing your own food, and have a think if you can source any second hand or upcycled alternatives.

When you reach the end of your first growing season, make a note of how it went, referring to the box on the next page.

Checklist

Have your notebook and pencil handy to make a note of your answers to the following prompts:

→ This year I want to try to grow . . .

→ My favourite crop to grow so far has been . . .

→ The fruit or vegetable that has tasted the best is . . .

→ I must list everything I have grown and work out how much money I have saved.

→ What crops did not go to plan?

→ This month I have harvested . . .

→ I must go to my local supermarket and work out how many air miles I have saved.

→ What shall I to try to grow next year?

→ What has caused the most damage to my crops (could be weather, animals, insects or anything else)?

3

Waste not,
want not!

'**Waste not, want not**' as my great-grandmother used to say! But what did she mean by this? Put simply, if you use a commodity or resource carefully and without excess, you will never be in need of it. This is arguably never more important than with food and water, the cornerstones of our very existence, plus two commodities our gardens can really contribute to.

Having spent the last chapter talking about how we can use our gardens, big and small, to help the global food supply chain by growing a few crops at home, it is now equally important that we understand how to store, preserve and use this food properly. As well as how to grow it in a water-wise and eco-friendly way.

I usually find growing the food to be the easy part, but the storage and preservation of it a bit more of a challenge. After all, I come from a generation where if something goes rotten, not to worry, you can simply pop to the store and buy another one, imported from who knows where!

One of my only regrets is not spending more time learning about this topic from my great-grandmother. I absorbed a wealth of gardening and growing knowledge from her, but I always lost interest as a child when it came to the storing and preserving part. I could never see the point of doing so, as the supermarket was only five minutes down the road, and packed full of all the pickles and jams you could ever need. It was not until after she died, I realized the error of my ways.

Growing up in the UK, I have sometimes taken the importance of fresh food for granted, because for my life so far at least it has been so readily available. Not so long ago fresh food was treasured as the valuable commodity that it is, and as such it was treated that way, as there was no option to bring in vast quantities that had been grown abroad. Harvests had to be looked after, as often that was all you had until the following year's harvest.

Unfortunately, over the last century, that appreciation for food has slowly eroded away, and as a consequence, a lot of the knowledge of how to make the most of this most valuable resource has been lost along with it. The good news is that with a little bit of research, and trial and error, we can soon pick up the ways of yesteryear, and bring back the good old-fashioned pantry or store-cupboard and fill it with preserved and properly stored fresh foods. We have the advantage of a few modern inventions to make this even easier and a more fun experience. Once the bug of learning how to store and preserve your food bites, it won't be long until your shelves are full of delicious homemade goodies. I find it comparable to home baking but with a greater sense of achievement, as you know you are doing your part to reduce waste while making good use of your amazing homegrown produce.

Growing fruit and vegetables at home is fantastic and something we should all consider doing, but often you will end up with what is known as a glut. This tends to happen in the late summer, when all your spring and summer crops will be ready to harvest, and you will find yourself in a position where, unless you need to feed a family of five hundred, it is easy to let a lot go to waste. Finding a quick and effective way to store this food is crucial. Correctly storing your crops is the easiest way to reduce your food waste, and as a result help other humans and the environment as a whole.

Why is food waste so important?

There are more of us than there have ever been on our planet, and this number is only expected to keep rising in the near future. More humans mean more mouths to feed, and with our current heavily flawed food chain and wasteful attitude this may prove to be a slight challenge. Unfortunately, most of the resulting hardship will fall onto the poorest in society, when often they have never been the cause of the problem in the first place.

Some level of food waste is inevitable. I have been guilty of letting food go mouldy, or being deterred by best-before dates (which are often complete rubbish, I might add), as I am sure nearly every single person reading this has. The problem lies not with a little bit of kitchen waste here and there, but with the current level of excess waste.

Every year enough food to feed three billion people is wasted. That is staggeringly nearly thirty per cent of all the food that is produced! Now this could be due to issues at the farming stage, processing stage, buying stage or storage in our homes. My guess is it is a pretty good mix of all of these. Regardless of the cause, this statistic really motivated me to rethink my relationship with food at home and see what changes I could make to address and prevent some of my own food waste.

I would just like to quickly share a story to highlight the food waste issue.

Not too far from where I live there is a soft fruit farm. This farm supplies soft fruits to a couple of the major UK supermarkets. All throughout the summer, you can spot these giant piles, which are often covered in swarms of flies and rodents. Inside these piles are the fruits deemed to be imperfect, and not fit for the supermarket shelves. Not composted, not set aside to be made into jams, not even sold off cheaply. Instead, it is just left in a giant heap to rot. Now for me, this was all the motivation I needed to start growing my own soft fruits, and as we explored in the last chapter this is actually easier than you might imagine. Happily, some stores and business have started to pick up and use these wonky veggies, but the practice of discarding some crops is still all too common.

Food waste is not just about fixing the issue of helping to feed the human population, it actually goes a whole lot wider. A lot of food waste is left to rot, usually in landfill, where it creates methane, a harmful greenhouse gas. Looking even wider, food waste not only wastes the food itself, but also the vast amount of energy and resources such as water, fertilizer, pesticides and sometimes even the energy from artificial light and heat used to grow and produce the food.

Enough doom and gloom! I think by now we all understand this is a bit of an issue and an important one at that. So, let's have a look at how we can make this situation better with a few very small changes and learning a few new fun and exciting skills to make the most of every bit of food we grow in our gardens or buy in the shops. Learning to store and preserve our food is not the only way we can help. Every garden, big or small, has a few tricks up its sleeve which we will also explore to help us on our journey to reduce food and water waste. By getting a little bit creative and utilizing the power of our gardens, they really can become nature's very own natural recycling plant!

Learn to store your produce

Learning how to store fresh produce can be a minefield of confusing and conflicting information, so let's unravel this tangled mess together. Proper storage of your fresh fruits and veggies is one of, if not *the* easiest way to reduce your food waste. Popular belief can be to pop all fresh produce in the fridge, but that is not always the answer.

Generally, the advice in this section applies to both store-bought and homegrown produce, but please bear in mind that for some crops this will be slightly different as some store-bought crops will need to ripen at home whereas homegrown are usually best left to ripen on the plant. However, the vast majority of guidance applies to both.

If you stop and think about just how much time, water, space and energy has gone into growing your produce, the least we can do is take a few easy steps to store it properly to avoid it going to waste.

There is not a one-size-fits-all rule for storing fresh produce, and the rules can even be different for storing the same produce at differing stages of ripeness. It might seem a bit daunting to start off, but soon it will become second nature, and just another part of unloading your shopping or storing those baskets of freshly harvested food.

> **Important note**
> *Throughout this section I refer to a crisper drawer. This is simply the drawer in your fridge, often at the bottom under the shelves, where you can keep produce separate from the rest of the contents within the fridge.*

So how do you store your fresh produce? Obviously, I cannot detail every product, so here I have handpicked a few of what I believe to be the most popular ones. By all means, experiment and learn what works best for you, but these are my recommendations.

I refer to cool dark places, and crisper drawers and fridges throughout this section. It is worth just adding a note on the temperatures I keep each one of these at in my own home so you can use it as a guide. Cool dark places such as storage cupboards and pantries, I keep between 10 and 20°C (50 and 68°F), and I keep my fridge and fridge crisper drawer at 4°C (40°F).

Apples

Apples are quite a complex one. Certain varieties that have been homegrown and stored wrapped in newspaper in a cool dark location will keep for months. However, for the majority of store-bought apples, keep them uncovered on your counter out of direct sunlight. You can also wrap them in a paper towel and place them in a paper bag with holes in it. Popped into your fridge crisper drawer, they will keep for nearly two months.

Asparagus

I like to store my asparagus spears in water. Fill up a cup or glass with fresh clean water, trim a few centimetres (at least an inch) off the bottom of the spears and place them in this water.

It is a good idea to change the water every other day to keep it fresh. These should be fine left on a countertop for two weeks. Alternatively, asparagus can be left in the crisper in your fridge, where they will last for a few days before the taste starts to fade. Asparagus has such a short growing season that they are usually only available for a month or two in spring. The best way to keep asparagus fresh and delicious is to respect this growing season, and look forward to that short period each year where they are a real treat!

Aubergines/eggplants

Aubergines are a bit of a contentious one! Some people swear by refrigerating them, and others say leave in a cool dark place such as a pantry. I ran a small trial and leaving in the pantry came out slightly on top. In all honesty aubergines are not great storers and need to be either used within six days or preserved using one of the methods discussed later in this chapter.

Avocados

The best way to store an unripe avocado is to keep it on a countertop, whole, and away from any other produce. Once your avocado ripens, pop it into the crisper drawer of your fridge, where it should last for around a week or so, as long as it is kept away from other ripe fruits, such as apples and bananas, as these can speed up the ripening process. Once sliced open, avocados will soon turn brown; to slow this you can squeeze a few drops of lemon on top, but it will still need to be consumed within a day or two.

Bananas

It is best to keep ripe bananas away from other fruits and vegetables as they release large amounts of ethylene gas, which can speed up the ripening process of surrounding produce. Store in a cool dry place, away from direct sun, and you can expect your bananas to last for seven to ten days. You may have read about covering the top with foil, but in my tests this made little difference.

Beetroot

Chop off the leafy green section, leaving just the bulb of the beetroot. Do not throw away these stems and leaves as they are fantastic when cooked with a little oil and garlic or eaten as a salad. Keep the skin of the bulb intact and store in your fridge crisper drawer. You can also store beetroot in layers of moist sand in a box, in a frost-free dark place, where they can be stored for up to two months.

Berries

Wash your berries in water and apple cider vinegar in a 3:1 ratio, and then thoroughly dry them by placing a paper towel on a plate and gently shaking the plate until all the berries are dry. Place a single layer of berries in a container, lined with paper towels and holes for airflow. Pop this container on a shelf in your fridge. You can skip the vinegar wash stage completely if you are worried about it distorting the taste, but your berries will need washing before you eat.

Carrots

Remove the green leafy tops of your carrots, but keep these to use as a brilliant basil substitute in homemade pesto. Avoid washing the carrots, and wrap each carrot in a dry paper towel. Place these in an airtight food container or bag and place in a cool fridge for up to three weeks. You can also try to store your carrots in sand, much the same way you can store beetroot, and they can store for up to a month.

Celery

Place your whole celery in the middle of some kitchen foil and wrap it up, making sure none of the celery is left exposed. Place this in your fridge and it will remain nice and crispy for two to three weeks. Please make sure to reuse the foil as many times as possible to cut down on waste.

Cherries

Store your cherries in the fridge. It is best to use an open container and avoid washing them until you are going to eat them. By doing this they can stay fresh for up to ten days.

Cucumbers

Wash your cucumbers – it is essential they are thoroughly dried after-wards– then wrap them in a dry paper towels and place in a plastic bag, but leave this unsealed to allow some airflow. Once this is done, pop this into the crisper drawer of your fridge where they can last for up to two weeks.

Herbs

There are two main categories of herbs, soft leafy herbs such as parsley, mint, coriander and basil, and hardier herbs such as rosemary, sage and oregano. To store softer herbs, fill a glass with few centimetres (an inch or two) of water, and place the stems into the water making sure none of the leaves is submerged. Remember to change the water every few days to make sure it remains fresh. Some herbs, such as basil, will actually grow roots and can be re-planted. The best way to store hardier herbs is to wrap them in a moist paper towel, then seal in an airtight container or sealable bag. Pop this in the fridge and check the paper towel every few days, to make sure it stays damp.

Garlic and onions

If you're harvesting homegrown garlic and onions, make sure to leave the green stems attached to the bulb. Then lay them on a drying rack so air can flow underneath, and leave to dry in a cool location. Once they have dried, they can be braided together and hung from the stems in a dry place such as a pantry or shed, where they can keep for two or three months. To store shop-bought garlic and onions, keep outside the fridge in a cool place, away from direct sunlight. Place sliced onion in a resealable bag and keep in the fridge, but use these within a week.

Ginger

To stop your ginger starting to shrivel, place it in an airtight sealed plastic bag and store in your fridge, ideally in the crisper section, where it can stay fresh for up to a month.

Grapes

Pop your grapes in a container with ventilation to allow airflow (often the punnet they came in is perfect for this), and place in the crisper drawer of your fridge for a week or two. Only wash them immediately before eating.

Lettuce and leafy greens

Lettuce is a tricky crop to store, and is always best eaten as soon as possible. Homegrown lettuce will often need a wash with clean water before bringing inside, as it can harbour quite a few insects, but be aware that by doing this you will reduce the shelf life. To store your lettuce, wrap it in a dry paper towel, pop in a plastic bag, and keep in the crisper drawer of your fridge. This can extend the life of your lettuce for a few more days.

Mushrooms

If you have grown your own mushrooms, or bought them loose from the shops, the best way to store them is in a brown paper bag lined with paper towels. Keep the bag open as the airflow will help prevent a build-up of moisture. Store your bag of mushrooms in the fridge for up to two weeks.

Peppers

To store fresh peppers, simply keep them in your fridge's crisper drawer. There is no need to wrap them or place in a container. If you have bought packaged store-bought peppers, you can leave them in the packaging until they are needed. Raw peppers should last for at least a week or two in the fridge.

Potatoes

It can be tempting to wash the dirt off your homegrown potatoes, but please avoid doing this as it can hamper their ability to store well. Homegrown potatoes can happily be stored in the soil for as long as three or four months for some varieties, but remember the longer they are in the ground, the higher the risk of damage from pests and disease. Homegrown and store-bought potatoes will do best stored in a cool dark place such as a pantry or cellar where they can be stored for up to two months.

Pumpkins and winter squash

When storing homegrown pumpkins and winter squash it is important to cure them. This can be achieved by simply leaving them out in the sun, for around ten days, covering them up during any colder nights. You can skip this stage for shop-bought pumpkins and winter squash, as they will be cured before reaching the shops. Store in a well-ventilated position between 10 and 20°C (50 and 68°F). Some varieties of winter squash can store for up to six months, but make sure to regularly check for signs of damage or bruising as this can soon lead to rot.

Strawberries

There are quite a few opinions surrounding how to store your strawberries at home. I have tried so many varied methods, such as vinegar baths and removing the green tops. The method that came out on top is to line a container with a dry paper towel and pop a single layer of strawberries into this. Then pop the lid back on and store the container of strawberries on a shelf in your fridge, and they should stay fresh for up to a week.

Tomatoes

When I am growing tomatoes at home, I prefer to leave them on the vine, until they are completely ripe, but if you have bought slightly unripe tomatoes from the shops, or you have unripe tomatoes growing in the garden and that first frost is fast approaching, it is best to harvest, and leave them on your counter tops for a few days to ripen. Once you have ripe tomatoes, they can be left on your kitchen counter tops if you plan on using them within a few days, or pop these loose in the crisper drawer of your fridge to keep fresh for a week or two.

One bad apple certainly can spoil the bunch!

I am sure we have all heard the saying, one bad apple can spoil the bunch. Well, there is actually a lot of truth to this, and in reality, it is not just confined to apples!

Please bear with me as I need to quickly take us back to the science classroom, just for a sentence or two. When certain fruits and vegetables ripen, they produce a gas called ethylene, which is often referred to as the fruit-ripening gas. This is a completely natural process as it helps the fruits to ripen. Producing ethylene is fine when apples are nice and spaced apart, growing on an apple tree out in the open air, but it can become a bit of a problem when we store our fruits at home.

Apples, bananas, cantaloupes, tomatoes and avocados are all great examples of fruits and veggies that all release a lot of ethylene. When these are stored next to other fruits and vegetables, this will often help to accidently trigger their ripening process, causing them to ripen faster than they normally would. It is important to be aware of this process, as it is why for these fruits and vegetables, the fruit bowl or same compartment in the fridge may not be the best option for storage. Premature overripening, caused by ethylene, can be easily avoided by just keeping high-ethylene-producing fruits and vegetables separate from ethylene-sensitive fruits and vegetables. A great example of how you can do this, and a tool I would recommend is a banana cradle. This allows you to separate your bananas in a neat way, away from other fruits and vegetables.

Ethylene is not all bad, though. You can use this process to your advantage to speed up the ripening of any unripe fruits and vegetables you may have. I sometimes like to store my semi-ripe tomatoes next to my apples in a container, and this can double the rate at which they ripen.

So just which fruits and vegetables produce a lot of ethylene and which ones are sensitive to it? Opposite is a quick check list you can use when deciding where to store your produce:

High ethylene producers	Ethylene sensitive
Apples	Banana
Bananas	Broccoli
Cantaloupe melon	Brussels sprouts
Tomatoes	Carrots
Avocados	Cabbage
Peaches	Cauliflower
Pears	Cucumbers
Apricots	Aubergine
Figs	Watermelon
Kiwi	Peppers
Plums	Green beans
Passion fruit	Peas

Top picks for a long shelf life

Not too long ago, people had to plan what they needed to grow in the summer months, in order to store and make them last throughout the autumn and winter months. Traditionally this was usually a lot of root vegetables, winter squash and pumpkins. Now, with the luxury of supermarkets, this is no longer a necessity, but it may be something we may want to consider in our gardens. I like to grow an excess of root vegetables such as carrots, parsnips, turnips and potatoes, as well as pumpkins and winter squash, as these will happily store long into the winter. There is something special about heading out into my storage compartment in the garden shed and selecting veggies to use that were homegrown during the previous summer. My goal every year is to try to cook Christmas dinner using mainly homegrown produce. This is certainly not easy, but by growing an excess of good storing crops in the summer, it is definitely possible.

This small selection of good storing crops, stashed away in a section of my shed, allows me to supplement my winter food shops. This in turn allows me to cut back on buying winter food that has often travelled thousands of miles, usually wrapped in plastic packaging, only for it to taste bland most of the time as it has been grown out of season. As seen in the previous chapter, it is possible to grow vast quantities of food at home, by using only a very small section of your garden or balcony.

Ten tips for longer storage:

1. Bring your produce inside as soon as possible after harvesting to avoid the heat wilting them (unless you are drying them, as with onions and garlic).

2. Keep fruits and vegetables out of direct sunlight once ripe.

3. Make good use of the crisper drawer in your fridge, it is designed specifically for fresh produce.

4. Try to avoid damaging the crop when harvesting and handling, as damaged produce will often spoil faster.

5. Some vegetables, such as garlic, onions, potatoes and squash, will do better in a cool, dark place.

6. Remove any rotten produce from the rest – the old saying one bad apple will spoil the bunch is true.

7. Try storing some crops in water; some, such as spring onions and basil, will even start to regrow.

8. Some crops, such as potatoes and parsnips can be stored in the soil where they are growing. Just be careful as the longer they are in the soil the more prone to insect and disease damage they become.

9. In general, it is best to avoid washing the produce until you are ready to use them. If you do wash, make sure to thoroughly dry before storing.

10. Share the harvests with friends and family to avoid any unnecessary waste.

Different ways to preserve your crops

Proper storage of your crops is only one solution to make the most of your harvest. Learning how to preserve your fresh homegrown crops, and even your store-bought fresh produce, is a valuable skill that should be in every gardener's arsenal. I would even go as far to say it should possibly find a place in the school curriculum as a life skill everyone should learn as a child. Teaching children to not waste food, but leaving out any solutions for them, seems counter-productive to me. Having said that, it is a skill I picked up later in life, so it is never too late to learn and my only regret is not doing so sooner!

Learning the different methods of how you can preserve your crops will undoubtedly help to decrease your food waste, and is also a valuable tool to deal with the inevitable glut of homegrown produce that comes at the end of each summer. While this section is primarily aimed at preserving homegrown produce, you can also buy and preserve fresh fruits and vegetables, from shops and farmers markets, at a time when they are in season, to store and use when they are out of season. They will often still taste better than bland out-of-season 'fresh' produce, and will also save a large number of air miles, and reduce the amount of artificial heat and light sometimes needed to grow out of season.

A few hours preserving food is such a great way to spend a Sunday afternoon, and also a great way to get family and friends involved. The sense of satisfaction I get from seeing my pantry full of homegrown or fresh produce, which has been carefully preserved using various methods and stored away for the more barren months, is as big, if not bigger, as when I harvest the produce in the first place.

There are so many ways to preserve your food at home, in fact I could easily write a whole book just on this topic. However, for the purpose of this chapter, we will focus on a few of the main methods, which are: freezing, fermenting, pickling, drying and bottling. We will also only be focusing on fruit, vegetables and herbs, and not meat, dairy or fish.

Getting started

Preserving your food can seem daunting for beginners, but in reality, it is actually very simple. After all, humans have been using some of the more ancient techniques, such as drying and fermenting, for thousands of years, and with a few modern inventions such as the freezer, it is easier than it has ever been. Naturally there are a few small risks when preserving food, but I have compiled some rules to keep these risks to a minimum.

My top tips for home preserving:

* All utensils and surfaces need to be clean and sterile.

* It is best to preserve your produce as soon after harvesting as possible, as this is when they will be perfectly ripe.

* Avoid using damaged, underripe or overripe produce, although these can sometimes be used for jams and chutneys.

* Make sure you label what is in each jar or bag as the appearance can often change during the preserving process, leading to confusion later on.

* Date each preserved package so you know how old each one is. This allows you to easily track when each preserved food is ready or which one to use first.

* If you are unsure if your preserved food is still safe to eat, it is best to avoid it, as sometimes the preserving method can fail due to broken seals or various other malfunctions.

* Test your equipment regularly. Damaged seals or chipped glass can often result in a bad batch of preserved food.

Now we have our top tips for preserving success, let's dive straight in, and learn how we can use each method and for which fruit and vegetables. Over time you will learn what works best for each crop, but while you are learning, play around and experiment, your tastes might be completely different to mine, and that is the beauty of preserving your own food.

Freezing

Freezing as a means of preserving food is still a relatively new method. While some preserving methods have thousands of years of history, home freezing has only become mainstream in the last fifty years.

Freezing is by far the easiest method of preserving your food at home, but please remember the cost and energy usage involved in keeping your freezers at these low temperatures. Buying a dedicated freezer to store your crops may not be the most eco friendly or cost-effective option, but if you have a connected fridge-freezer, then it makes sense to utilize this option as you are using the energy regardless.

What can you freeze?

Some crops are better suited to home freezing than others; for example, I regularly freeze garden peas and beans, but I would not freeze a potato, pumpkin or squash, as these, if kept whole, can happily store for months at a time without the help of a freezer. I always like to avoid any leafy greens such as lettuce as well as cucumbers since their high-water content makes them far from ideal for home freezing.

It is important to think about what you want to eventually use the crop for when deciding if you want to freeze it. A great example of this is tomatoes. Every year I grow basket after basket of tomatoes, and inevitably have to preserve some. The tomatoes that end up in the freezer are great when in the future they are destined to be cooked down into dishes such as lasagne or blended into a tomato sauce. They will not be as good, however, if you wish to defrost, and use them as a chopped tomato in a salad, as you will most likely end up with a bit of a mushy mess, with the odd piece of crunchy iced flesh mixed in. Drying and dehydrating is, for me, a better option for preserving tomatoes for a salad.

Fruits, especially soft fruits, can be successfully frozen, but it is a similar story to tomatoes. They will be fantastic when blended into smoothies, but I would avoid eating a bowl of defrosted strawberries. If you wish to eat them as whole strawberries at a later date, I would choose to dehydrate them instead.

How to freeze your crops

This does not need to be complex; some guides will give you many different fancy packing techniques and washes, etc, but I like to just keep it simple.

First make sure you are using ripe and unblemished crops; any overripe or slightly damaged crops are best eaten straight away, or made into jams and sauces. Give your produce a good wash with fresh water and then dry it.

Now some produce will need to be blanched before being frozen. Blanching is essentially lightly boiling your produce for a short period of time, usually a couple of minutes, and then immediately cooling them in a bowl of cold water to stop the cooking process. As a general rule, vegetables you would normally eat cooked, such as broccoli, need a quick blanch before freezing, whereas crops you normally eat raw, such as tomatoes, do not.

It is always a good idea to prepare your veggies before freezing rather than freezing them whole, as you want them ready to use straight from the freezer. So, peel and slice vegetables such as carrots, remove peas from their pods and slice up runner beans into bite-size chunks. This is far easier to do before blanching. When it comes to storing your crops, a sealable freezer bag, or small sealed containers will work fine, just make sure to keep reusing these containers to avoid waste.

Unlike meat and fish, fruit and veggies are normally best used without defrosting, and instead cooked or blended straight from their frozen state.

My top picks to freeze

As mentioned most produce is suitable for home freezing, but here are my favourites:

* Garden peas, lightly blanched for a couple of minutes without the pods they grow in.

* Runner beans chopped into 2–3 cm (about an inch) segments and blanched for three minutes.

* French beans prepared in the same way as runner beans.

* Broad beans without the pods they grow in – I prefer not to blanch broad beans.

* Sweetcorn without the green husks, and the cob chopped into more manageable 7–10 cm (3–4 in) sections.

* Tomatoes to be used in cooking or sauces.

* Chillies frozen whole, which are best used in cooking or sauces.

* Broccoli broken into small florets.

* Cauliflower broken into small florets.

* Grapes to be used as ice cubes in drinks. Simply freeze whole or half grapes, then once they are frozen you can add these to your cold drinks as an ice cube that you can also eat.

* Carrots peeled and sliced, or cut into batons or diced, whichever is your favourite.

* Whole soft fruits such as strawberries, raspberries, currants and blueberries to be used in cooking or blended into smoothies.

Drying and dehydrating

Drying is one of the most common and oldest methods of preserving food. Whether it was the Romans and their dried fruits, such as figs and grapes, or the Nordic clans and their dried fish, humans have been drying food for a very long time. Fast forward a few thousand years and we now have faster and more reliable drying techniques and tools; however, you can still dry naturally using the older techniques, to save money and conserve energy.

Drying is one of the more beginner-friendly methods of preserving, since we are quite familiar with how dried foods, especially fruits, should look as they are widely available in shops. Quite often it involves simply leaving finely sliced fruits and vegetables, in stable conditions, until they have lost most of their internal moisture. Dehydrating food essentially works by reducing its moisture content, down to usually between five and twenty per cent. Within this range the bacteria that causes food decay struggles to survive, allowing the food to last for far longer than it would normally.

What can you dehydrate?

Dehydrating is more usual for the preservation of fruits and herbs than vegetables, with the exception of onions, garlic, chillies, mushrooms and tomatoes. Dehydrated vegetables such as celery and carrots, are fantastic if blended and added to hot water to make a natural vegetable stock. So, as with freezing, it is important to think about what you would like to use that crop for in the future before selecting a method of preservation to use.

Just like freezing, dehydrating is an option for most fruits, veggies and herbs, but it is best to again avoid those with a high water content such as lettuce and cucumbers, as they will not dry very well, and often the moisture is what provides most of the flavour for these crops.

When dehydrating food, it is important to use blemish-free, ripe crops. If you are trying to dry fruits but you think they are slightly overripe, you can use these to make fruit leather instead. This is easily achieved by blending the fruit with a little added sugar until it is smooth. Then spread a very thin layer onto a non-stick surface such as greaseproof paper. This can be placed in your oven on a very low heat or into a purpose-built dehydrator.

How to dehydrate your crops?

As mentioned earlier, there are a few ways you can dehydrate your crops by using both artificial and natural methods. If you are lucky enough to live in a warm sunny climate, the easiest way to dehydrate is to use the sun, whereas if like me you live in a more unsettled climate, it is easier to air dry or use artificial methods such as your oven or a dehydrator.

Preparing your crops to dehydrate is simple. All you need to do is give them a good wash with clean water and then thoroughly dry them. I recommend you remove the skins on fruits such as apples and pears. The key to success with dehydrating is to make sure you slice your crops into thin sections, usually no more than 1 cm (½ in) thick. The more consistent you get these slices, the better the end result will be. Not all produce needs to be thinly sliced, for example, many people like to dehydrate grapes whole to create raisins, but the thicker the fruit or vegetable, the longer it will take to dehydrate, and when dehydrating using a dehydrator or oven, the less cost-or energy-efficient it will be.

Place your thinly sliced produce onto a cooling rack, which has the ability to let the air flow all the way around as well as underneath. The metal bars inside your oven are perfect for this, or you can purchase special drying racks, which if you plan on drying a lot, I would highly recommend.

To dry in the sun, place this tray outside in direct sun, but make sure you cover it with a fine-mesh net to avoid insects landing on and spoiling your produce. Sun drying is only really effective once the heat is above 30°C (86°F), so for the vast majority of people it is only really an option during the midsummer months. It is important to turn your fruits or vegetables every few hours, and make sure to protect them overnight, otherwise the local wildlife will enjoy your food. After a few days of baking in the sun, stack up your trays and place them in the shade, but please make sure there is still a good level of airflow. They should remain here until they resemble a leathery texture. Sun-dried food is great and will save the use of energy, but it can be quite a prolonged process. Insects will inevitably come along to see what they can steal, so make sure your produce is covered with a fine mesh. When sun drying it is important to have a long spell of sunny, warm and consistent weather, which can be little bit of a challenge in my UK climate.

Another low-energy method of dehydrating is to air dry. Please be aware this is not an option for all produce, as I have found out the hard way! Air drying is my go-to method for chillies, but avoid juicy crops such as strawberries as they tend to just go mouldy in these conditions. The key to success with air drying, is to hang your crops, suspended from a string or thread, in an area of your house where the air is dry. Airing cupboards and boiler spaces are a great option, as is the kitchen, but avoid warm, humid rooms such as the bathroom. The only crops I recommend for this method are herbs, such as lavender, oregano and thyme; and onions, shallots, garlic and chilli peppers.

My favourite crop to air dry is chillies. Using a needle and thread, poke the thread through the end of your chillies, and slide them all the way down to a knotted end. Suspend your chilli strings in a warm dry area with good airflow.

After a month or so, they will have dehydrated and will happily store for many months, plus I think they also make a really cool decoration for your kitchen.

Both of these ancient techniques undoubtedly work, but for me the easiest and most effective way to dry is to use your oven or to purchase a dehydrator. If your oven temperature can go as low as 50–65°C/122–149°F, then you can effectively use your oven to dehydrate most produce in usually only an hour or two. However, if your oven cannot effectively be reduced to that temperature, it is a good idea to consider purchasing a dehydrator. The initial cost can seem high, but my dehydrator has paid for itself multiple times over thanks to the amount of food it has prevented from going bad. The energy consumption is lower than an oven, and all you have to do is load in your produce, set the timer and temperature, then click start. After a few hours you will have beautifully dehydrated food that has taken very little effort to make.

Dehydrated food does not need to be stored in an airtight container, like most other preserved foods. Just make sure it is stored in a cool, dry place that is not too humid.

Another great way to dry your produce is by freeze drying. This has seen a recent surge in popularity, and freeze-dried fruits are now quite common in shops. The reason I haven't discussed it here, is simply because the equipment is only really available on an industrial scale, and is very expensive to purchase.

My top crops to dehydrate

I find fruits and herbs are far more suited to dehydrating than the vast majority of vegetables, and here are my top picks:

* **Apples:** I like to remove the core of the apple and peel away the skin, then slice the apple into rings no thicker than 1 cm (½ in). You can also use a potato peeler to peel away thin strips of apple flesh to dry.

* **Apricot:** Simply slice your apricots in half, remove the stones and dry each half of the apricot, there is no need to slice into really thin sections.

* **Banana:** Peel and chop your banana into thin discs around 1 cm (½ in) thick, the thinner they are the faster they will dry.

* **Chillies:** Please see page 77.

* **Figs:** Dried figs are amazing! While they can be dried whole, it is much easier to cut the fig horizontally into 1 cm (½ in) thick slices.

* **Garlic:** The same process as onions.

* **Grapes:** Grapes are commonly dried whole to create raisins.

* **Lavender:** The same process as oregano.

* **Mango:** Peel and slice your mango into long but very thin – only 0.5 cm (¼ in) thick – strips. I like to aim for at least the length of the whole mango. To achieve this, you can peel the mango flesh with a potato peeler.

* **Mushrooms:** Smaller mushrooms can be dried whole, but for larger mushrooms, slice into 1 cm (½ in) thick slices. When it comes to using dried mushrooms, they are best rehydrated by placing in a bowl of hot or cold water for 10 minutes before using.

* **Onions:** Peel and dice your onions, into small 1–2 cm (½–¾ in) chunks. These will add a nice crunch to any meal.

* **Oregano:** Simply tie the stalks together and hang in an area of your home, or shed if you have one, that is not too humid and has good airflow. After a few weeks your oregano will be nice and dry.

* **Pineapple:** Peel away the skin and remove the core as this is too hard to dry (but makes amazing pineapple tea when boiled in water). From here you can slice or dice the

pineapple however you like. Just remember the thinner your slices, the faster they will dry.

* **Plums:** The same process as apricots.

* **Strawberries:** Small strawberries can be dehydrated whole, but I prefer to slice my strawberries into 1 cm (½ in) thick slices, as this requires less energy to dry.

* **Thyme:** The same process as oregano.

* **Tomatoes**: Tomatoes can be dried whole if they are small, or sliced into thin rings, or even just in half.

Fermenting food

Fermenting is the method of preserving food that often confuses and scares people. Before I started fermenting food at home, I fell into this camp too. However, once you start you will soon realize just how simple it really is, and your shelves will soon be filled with all sorts of weird and wonderful concoctions of different fermenting foods.

So just what is fermenting? Fermentation is an anaerobic process in which microorganisms such as yeast and bacteria start to break down food elements, such as sugars and carbohydrates, into other products like acids, gases and even alcohol.

There are quite a few different methods of fermenting food, but when we ferment vegetables, we are often using a method called lacto-fermenting. All vegetables have some lactic acid bacteria in or on them. Lactic acid bacteria are classed as a good bacteria, which will help support your gut microbiome. By fermenting food in brine, we are creating an environment where this good bacteria thrive, and the harmful bacteria can no longer survive. The goal here is to create a brine that is salty enough to kill off the bad bacteria, but not too salty, so the good bacteria can still survive. This might all sound complex, but in reality, it is all very simple to achieve.

Fermentation is one of the fastest and most beneficial methods of preserving foods. Fermented food can be ready in as little as three or four days, compared to the months it can take to pickle your produce. Fermenting is also a zero-energy way to preserve your food, as it requires no heat, light or cooling to work. However, by far the main benefit of fermentation is that is the only way of preserving food that actually makes it healthier than it is in its original form. This is due to the levels of probiotics, digestive enzymes and healthy acids that are created during the fermentation process.

What can you ferment?

You can ferment nearly all food types, including meats, fish and even some dairy products. However, we will focus only on fruits and vegetables in this chapter. You can ferment pretty much any fruits or vegetables, but as a general rule avoid fermenting vegetables you would usually need to cook, such as potatoes. These might need a slightly different method as the cooking process will kill off many of the good bacteria that are needed for successful fermentation. To ferment cooked vegetables, you will need to use a starter culture, which we are not going to cover here.

Play around and figure out what you like. For me, I really dislike fermented fruits, so I choose to dehydrate these instead, but I love fermented cabbage. Remember, there are no right or wrong options, it is down to your personal preference, and over time you will learn what methods of preserving you find best for each crop.

Having said that, avocados are one to avoid when fermenting as they will just turn to mush. The high concentration of sugars in tomatoes can make them problematic too.

How to ferment your crops

The key to success when fermenting is to make sure you use a sterile fermenting vessel. The most popular vessel, and my favourite, is a glass Mason jar, with a secure lid. To sterilize your jars, wash them with hot clean water and dry in your oven at 150°C (300°F), or alternatively in your microwave on full power for 90 seconds. You can opt to put your jars into the dishwasher, but many domestic dishwashers will not reach a high enough drying temperature to ensure the vessels have been properly sterilized.

Do not be afraid to mix produce to find different flavours that you enjoy. I love mixing carrots and garlic or beans and peppercorns, so just have a bit of an experiment and figure out what you like.

To get started simply chop up your produce so it will fit into your jar, and add in some spices for additional flavour, such as chilli flakes or peppercorns. It is a good idea to try to keep the chunks roughly the same size, so it all ferments at a similar speed. Next, we need to create our brine. It is really important to use kosher, Himalayan or pure sea salt, as regular table salt can kill the good bacteria. Add 5 g (1 tsp) salt to every 100 g (31.5 oz) of water, to create a 5% brine, and pour this into the jar, making sure all produce is submerged, but still leaving a 2.5 cm (1 in) gap at the top of the jar.

All the produce in the fermenting vessel needs to stay below the brine. If it comes into contact with the air this can cause mould. I like to use a fermenting weight to stop this from happening. These are usually glass cylinders that just slot into your fermenting vessel, and these can be bought in most kitchenware shops.

Close the lid to seal the jar, and store at room temperature for the next three days. It is wise to routinely burp the jar to release pressure and stop it from exploding. Your jar needs burping if you hear a hissing sound when you carefully unscrew the lid. To burp your jar, gently unscrew the lid until you hear a small hiss, and then once it stops quickly close it back up again. Start to taste your ferment after three days, and continue to taste until you find the flavour you like. Once you have the flavour you like simply store in a cool dark place.

If you are new to fermented foods, try to not eat too much in one go. Start with a few spoonfuls each day and build it up gradually over time.

The more you ferment the easier the process will become. Mould can form during the fermentation process. I am not comfortable eating this, even though some people say just scoop it out! If your ferment is mouldy, try again, but adjust your amount of salt in the brine to a slightly higher concentration.

Sauerkraut recipe

Two of the most popular fermented foods are kimchi and sauerkraut, and this simple twenty-minute recipe is a must try, and a great introduction into the world of fermented foods.

INGREDIENTS
2 kg (2½ lb) white cabbage
Sea salt, Himalayan or kosher salt
1 teaspoon caraway seeds
1 teaspoon peppercorns

METHOD:

* Start by washing four half-litre glass (18 fl oz) Mason jars with hot water, and place in an oven preheated at 180°C/350°F for around fifteen minutes to sterilize. Make sure all surfaces and utensils are clean.

* Shred the cabbage using a sharp knife or even a few pulses in your blender. Place in a large bowl.

* Massage around 5 tablespoons of salt into the cabbage for around five minutes, and let it sit for another ten. Repeat the massage two more times, without adding any more additional salt, and the resulting mixture should be reduced cabbage sitting in its own brine.

* Add the caraway seeds and peppercorns, and start to jar up your mixture, making sure to compress the cabbage below the liquid, and remember to use a weight to keep it below the brine.

* Release the gas in the jar for the next week and then leave it in a room-temperature place for the next five days. Your sauerkraut will be ready after a week but for the best flavours leave it for at least two.

* Once you have the flavour you like, transfer into smaller sterile jars and keep in the fridge, where it will be good to eat for up to six months.

Pickling your harvests

Pickling is my favourite way to preserve harvests. It is also one method of preserved food that we are all very familiar with, as pickled food is widely available in the shops. Pickled onions and gherkins are a favourite for many people, but there are so many other fantastic pickled recipes you can use to preserve your own food at home.

Pickling is essentially placing food in an edible liquid, usually vinegar, which has a low enough pH level that bad bacteria, and other microorganisms, can no longer survive. It is this presence of acid that differentiates pickling from fermenting, but the processes have many similarities.

The time needed to pickle produce can be longer than some other preserving methods, as many crops need to pickle for at least a month, with many achieving their best flavour after many more.

What can you pickle?

Most vegetables and fruits are suitable for home pickling, but this method of preservation tends to favour vegetables rather than fruits. However, having said that, pickled watermelon, yes watermelon, is becoming popular. Go wild, try pickling various crops and experiment with different spices and herbs. By pickling lots of different crops, you will learn what you enjoy and what you might want to avoid in the future. I usually choose to pickle crops that have a good firm structure to them, such as onions, garlic, cucumber and carrots, and avoid softer crops such as tomatoes, as they run the risk of going mushy during the pickling process.

You can pickle other food types such as eggs, meat and fish, but to align with the rest of this chapter we are going to focus on the home-grown fresh produce.

How to pickle your harvests

As with fermenting, the key to success with pickling is to make sure you are using clean and sterilized vessels, surfaces, tools and hands. Please follow the same sterilizing methods as mentioned in the previous fermenting section (see page 82).

Once you have chosen what produce you would like to pickle, decide if you need to cut it down to size, or pickle it whole. I usually pickle smaller varieties, so I often pickle whole, but some crops, such as beetroot, will usually need to be sliced. If you go down the slicing route, make sure to keep the sizes as even as possible.

Salt your produce in a brine mixture (I use the same 5% solution as for fermenting; see page 83) and weigh it down, so it remains completely covered. Leave your produce in this solution for 12 to 24 hours and then thoroughly rinse with clean water.

At this stage there are two main methods you can use: hot pickling and cold pickling, the latter being my favourite. To hot pickle you need to cook the produce and pack it into a hot jar, where near-boiling vinegar is added. For the vast majority of produce, I like to lightly blanch, to prevent anything from being overcooked, which can cause a mushy texture. To cold pickle, add your produce to a room-temperature jar, cover with room-temperature vinegar and seal with an airtight lid.

Store your pickles in a cool dark space, usually for at least one month – with the exception of cabbage and beetroot, as these need consuming within two months. When pickling crops such as onions and shallots, I find the flavour intensifies each month, and around six months is the sweet spot for me.

My top pickle picks

I find pickling works best when vegetables with a firmer structure are used, as they will not turn soft during the pickling process and will give you a wonderful crunchy texture. Please do not be scared of big bold flavours and spices. The pickling process will subdue these flavours, ever so slightly, making them less overpowering. I would not dream of chewing on a raw garlic clove, whereas pickled garlic is an hidden underrated gem! A few other must-tries are:

* **Asparagus:** This might sound odd, but it is surprisingly nice, just make sure you use young, small spears.

* **Beetroot:** Smaller beetroot can be pickled whole but slice larger ones into 3 cm (1¼ in) thick discs.

* **Cabbage:** This is usually best shredded; I achieve this by grating with the large side of a cheese grater.

* **Carrots:** Peel away the outer skin, and then slice into batons around 6 cm (2½ in) long. I find batons fit better in the jar than discs but that is just personal preference.

* **Cauliflower:** Chop it into small florets.

* **Chillies:** I pickle all of my chillies whole, but for any really big chillies simply slice into 2 cm (¾ in) thick discs.

* **Cucumbers:** If you have very small baby cucumbers no bigger than 10 cm (4 in) then you can pickle these whole; for larger ones, I recommend slicing into discs.

* **Garlic:** Skin removed and individual cloves separated and pickled.

* **Green beans:** Chop your beans in half, or if they are really long possibly into thirds (this doesn't have any impact on flavour, but rather simply helps them fit into the jar).

* **Onions:** Smaller onions will always work best; I like to pickle whole onions that are no larger than a golf ball.

* **Shallots:** The same process as onions.

Bottling and Canning

Technically, bottling refers to using a glass jar, whereas canning refers to using a tin can. However, for the purpose of this section, I will use both words to refer to the process of using a glass jar. In the UK we would normally call this bottling, but our friends in the USA often refer to this as canning.

Bottling has seen a massive surge in popularity during the last few years, with countless blogs and websites dedicated to just this method of preserving. Bottling is relatively straightforward, and the preserved food will often still resemble its appearance before the preservation. With the exception of freezing, this is quite rare in the world of preserves.

Bottling is essentially storing fruits and vegetables, in a vessel (usually a glass jar) covered with water, syrup or brine, and then sealed using heat, to prevent bacteria from entering. This sounds simple and as long as you follow the rules, it really is. Following the rules is important with all methods of preserving, especially those on cleanliness, but is arguably most important when bottling.

It is essential that all equipment and surfaces are sterile, especially your glass jars. Test your jars to make sure they are airtight and that the seals are intact. Please avoid using any chipped, dented or damaged jars. Wash them thoroughly with warm soapy water, then rinse and dry in the oven, which is heated to at least 150°C (300°F).

What can you bottle?

While you most certainly can bottle vegetables, fruits are often far easier and far more popular. This is mainly due to their higher acid content; a lower boiling temperature is needed.

How to bottle your harvests and in-season produce from the shops

As with most preserving methods, it is important to use perfectly ripe fruits, without any damage or blemishes. If you have damaged or blemished fruit, please use it first as a fresh option, or alternatively use fruits to make jams, and vegetables to make chutneys or sauces. Some fruits will need to be prepared before bottling. Often, this just involves peeling skins and removing the cores.

When bottling, my preferred liquid is syrup, as it enhances the flavour of the fruits. Syrup may not be the healthiest option, but it sure makes for a fantastic treat! To prepare your syrup, add 250 g (9 oz) to each 300 ml (10 fl oz) of water. Boil together for one minute, and then add the same amount of water again. Once you have added your water, heat until all of the sugar has dissolved.

Pop your prepared fruits into a sterilized jar. I find it easier to work with slightly larger jars, but the jar size will not make any difference to the bottling process. Pour in your syrup, and use a knife to carefully remove any air bubbles. Make sure you add enough syrup to fill the jar, leaving just a few centimetres (an inch or so) from the top.

Fill up a large pan with water and place in a false bottom (a round metal rack which can be purchased in kitchenware or charity shops) so the bottom of the jars will not be in contact with the bottom of the pan. Gently bring this water to a rolling boil. Place the jars into the water for the required heating time for that crop (for syrup, for example, if you are using a smaller jar under half a litre(18 fl oz), this is usually around 10 minutes in a rolling boil, and for jars between half a litre to a litre (18 to 35 fl oz)it is around 15 minutes). Once boiled remove from the water and tightly screw down your lids, to create a seal. Always label with what the content is and the date it was made, and store in a cool dark place.

My top picks to bottle/can

As mentioned earlier, bottling is far more suited to fruits than vegetables and here are my favourites for you to consider trying at home:

* Apples
* Pears
* Pineapple
* Cherries
* Grapes
* Plums

* Strawberries
* Peaches
* Apricots
* Watermelon
* Oranges

Other common methods of prolonging the shelf life of your crops

I would like to give a few honourable mentions to jams, chutneys, infused vinegars and salting. All of these are fantastic ways to preserve your food and I highly recommend that you research these further.

Compost, or garden gold, as it should be called!

Even when you are preserving your food, a level of organic waste is always unavoidable. You often need to peel, de-core or remove non-edible parts such as the vines on your tomatoes. Also, growing your own food or just having a garden in general will create a lot of organic garden waste. Composting is the garden's amazing way of recycling all of this organic waste, plus some brown wastes, such as paper and cardboard, to create a natural garden gold. The best part about composting is it requires very little financial outlay, and is possibly the easiest recycling you will ever do.

What is compost?

Put simply, compost is essentially a mixture of decomposing or decomposed organic material. Although, I prefer to think of compost as turning your garden waste and organic scraps into something of great value.

Over time, all organic matter will eventually break down, but by composting, we are essentially just speeding up this process so it is ready to use in our garden in months rather than years. By utilizing various different methods, we can create the best conditions for bacteria, fungi and other lifeforms, such as worms and microorganisms, to get to work.

So, just why is homemade compost important?

This is a bold statement, but composting could be most valuable activity you can do in your garden. Not only for your garden's health, but also the environment and your wallet. I could easily write a whole book on composting, but for now let's keep it simple, as this topic does not need to be over complicated.

As mentioned in the previous chapter (see page 38), good garden soil is essential if you want to grow the best crops and flowers possible. Homemade compost is the ideal natural way to add fertility and bring your garden soil to life. Due to all the rotted organic matter, garden compost is packed full of nutrients your plants will love, helping to boost the fertility of your soil, and as a result boosting the performance of your garden. Traditionally garden compost is made for that exact reason, but enriching your garden soil is only one of many great reasons why we should all think about composting at home. A few other great reasons to start composting include:

REDUCING PLASTIC AND FUEL USAGE

Us gardeners use a lot of compost, in fact last year it was predicted that over one hundred million bags were sold globally, and this number has been growing rapidly in recent years, with no sign of slowing down. Many of these compost bags are made out of a type of plastic that is very tricky to recycle, and even when they can be recycled, this takes a lot of energy to do successfully. Deciding to make compost yourself reduces the need and reliance on these store-bought plastic bags and is really the ultimate step in your garden becoming self-sufficient. Homemade compost has the added benefit of usually being made right where it is going to be used. Not only does this cut out all the fuel use to transport large heavy pallets filled with bags of compost, it saves you the back-breaking work of getting said compost from the store into your garden.

HELPING TO SAVE WATER

Water is one of the most valuable resources we have. I mean, without it we have a massive problem on our hands. Yes, homemade compost can often need some added water to work effectively, but this is nothing compared to the levels of water required to make the compost found in the stores. Plus, garden compost has brilliant water saving capabilities too, helping to dramatically reduce our water consumption, which is already strained. Homemade compost when added to sandy soil can help bind the particles together, increasing the moisture – holding capabilities and reducing the amount of water needed to grow crops and flowers. When sprinkled over your existing soil, garden compost not only adds nutrients, but acts as a fantastic mulch. This mulch will further help reduce the watering needs of the garden by locking in the moisture, meaning less is lost to evaporation.

REDUCING LANDFILL

No organic waste should ever find its way into landfill. However, unfortunately across the globe millions of tonnes of organic waste is destined to end up exactly there. This is problematic on so many levels, and honestly it breaks my heart. Organic waste ending up in landfill really is the ultimate waste, especially when nature has its very own easy and eco-friendly way of recycling it into such a valuable resource. If every garden had even the smallest compost heap, then very little organic waste would ever need to head to landfill. Instead, it could be repurposed back into our gardens to create more life. The main issue of organic waste finding its way into landfill is the amount of greenhouse gases it produces, specifically methane. We briefly touched on methane earlier. It is nasty gas that we should do our best to avoid where possible. Some level of methane will always be unavoidable, but methane emitted due to rotting organic matter in landfill, is completely unacceptable, and I have no clue why it is not controlled. Composting, on the other hand, is an aerobic process, which is different to the anaerobic process commonly found in landfill. The key point here is that the process of composting does not produce methane, as methane-producing microbes are not active due to the oxygen involved. As you will see later (see page 100) this is why it is essential to let air get into your compost heap, otherwise you will end up with a big, stinky, methane-producing pile of waste.

SAVING OUR PEATLANDS

Peat is a common ingredient in many composts sold in the shops. While peat-free alternatives are becoming more popular, they are still heavily outweighed by the peat options. Peat is extracted from peat bogs in vast quantities to be used in our compost mixes. This boggles my mind as it is an irreplaceable resource, and the level of harm its extraction does to the environment should be considered a crime. Peatlands are one of the most delicate and complex ecosystems, often home to plants and wildlife rarely found elsewhere. It takes hundreds of years to form, but only minutes to rip out. The destruction of the complex and fragile nature of peatlands is only one issue. Arguably, the even bigger issue is that of carbon dioxide. You see, peat is a fantastic carbon store, capturing it and locking it away, aiding us in our ongoing issue with climate change. However, once peat is ripped out and processed to be bagged and sold in our compost, all of that stored carbon dioxide is released, and there is the reduction in the overall levels of peat to help capture more carbon dioxide in the future. By simply making your own garden compost you can dramatically reduce the destruction of peatlands. This is such an important topic, that we will discuss it further later on in this chapter (see page 104).

HELPING TO SAVE YOU MONEY

I think it is fair to say we all enjoy saving money. As my great-grand-mother used to say, 'a penny saved is a penny earned', and that probably explains my love of saving a penny or two. The funny part about compost is it is practically free and easy to make at home, yet it is starting to cost a fortune to buy in the shops. The financial outlay to make homemade compost is practically zero, as you will soon see, yet companies are charging silly prices for a bag of often below-par compost. Sure, as we have discussed, homemade compost has many environmental benefits, but it is also important to look after our wallets too.

I understand some of you may be thinking you do not have a need for compost, so all of this is great, but I just do not need it. I completely appreciate this, however, there are plenty of others who would love to take this compost, or even just the ingredients to make the compost, off your hands. Head to any allotment, park or shared garden and people will be lining up to take your garden gold, as it is so valuable to us gardeners, and hey, if you are business minded, I am sure some people (myself included) would happily pay you for it too! So, before you skip to the next chapter, please maybe keep that in mind.

How do you make homemade compost?

There are so many amazing benefits of homemade compost, both on a horticultural and environmental level, I could talk about it for another five chapters! But, without knowing how to make it, it is all a bit redundant, so I'd better take a few pages to explain just how simple and easy this is to do. I know it may sound daunting, but I promise you, this is the easiest form of recycling you will ever do, and the sense of satisfaction you will get once it is done, is up there with harvesting your own fresh food!

When it comes to making homemade compost there are lots of methods you can utilize, however we will focus on the most popular two: hot composting and cold composting.

WHICH COMPOST BIN IS BEST FOR YOU?

Before you decide what method of composting you would like to use, it is important to first have a place to store your organic waste. Now you have quite a few options here, ranging from completely free to quite expensive. If you have a large garden, I would recommend building a wooden composter. The easiest way to do this is to screw four full-size wooden pallets, into a square, and you are done, yes it really is that easy. If you are lucky, you may be able to source free pallets too! Ideally you want your wooden composter to be at least one metre (3 feet) square, but if space is at a premium then smaller can work too. This is

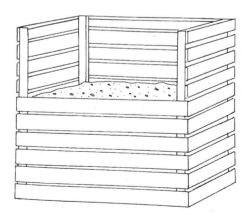

exactly what I have done at my allotment, it was completely free and works really well.

If you have a smaller garden or a balcony, then a closed compost bin is probably the best option. These can be bought relatively cheaply (some local governments even give them away for free), or you can try to find a second-hand one. They have an opening lid on the top to load your waste into, and a hatch near the bottom to check on its progress. This is the method I use in my garden as it keeps it nice and neat, plus it can really help to speed up the composting process as they usually get hotter as well.

Where space is at a real premium, your best option is to use a small compost bin. These are usually on a tumbling system, with a handle

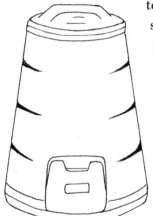

to help you turn the waste inside. These can be as small as a kitchen bin or you can select a slightly larger option. These are by far the most expensive option, but work well and are definitely the neatest.

It is important to keep your compost bin in an area of the garden where the temperature is pretty consistent. I like to place mine in partial shade, to prevent it from getting too hot in the summer months, which can cause it to dry out too fast.

Hot composting or cold composting?

Once you have decided which compost bin is best for your needs, you need to think about whether you would like to use cold composting or hot composting.

Cold composting is the slower of the two options, but it is the one that I use in my garden and allotment. Cold composting is by far the easiest method of turning all that organic waste into garden gold, as it requires very little input from you. To get your cold compost started, just fill your compost bin with organic waste, as and when it becomes available. Over time this bin will slowly fill up, and after around a year it will rot down to create compost. Cold composting does not require you to turn or attend to your compost, all you need to do is fill it up and just make sure it does not dry out.

Hot composting involves filling your compost bin all the way to the top, with a mix of organic and brown waste, all in one go, or over a day or two, and then using a fork to turn the heap every week, so it all starts to rot and build up heat. Hot composting is by far the fastest method, with your compost being ready in as little as three to six months. Hot composting is a great method, but for me there are a few issues. The first problem is you need a lot of organic waste all at once for it to work, and unless you have a very large garden, it is quite hard to achieve this. But for me, the main issue is that life is simply too short to spend time each and every week turning the compost heap. Yes, by turning it you will speed up the process, but for me waiting a few months longer for my compost has never caused any issues.

WORMERIES AND LEAF MOULD

There are some alternative methods of composting that are worth mentioning here too. If you have large amounts of organic kitchen waste, and only small amounts of garden waste, then a wormery might be a good option. A wormery is usually a container with two layers: a top layer for the organic waste and a bottom layer where the worms operate. You can add in all the regular ingredients we will discuss on page 101, but try to avoid citrus and onions as the worms are not too fond of these. It is important to remember composting worms are different to earth worms, so you will need to go out and buy some, rather than collecting them from your garden. Wormeries will work fast, and as well as providing you with compost (or worm castings) you will get a bonus liquid feed for your plants too. The major downside of wormeries is they can be a little bit smelly and can often only process small amounts of waste at a time.

Fallen autumn leaves can be added to your compost bin, but they are better turned into leaf mould, as they often decompose more slowly than the rest of the other organic waste, leading to big lumps of half-decomposed leaves in your compost. Creating leaf mould is super easy, all you need to do is collect some fallen autumn leaves and pop them in some bags. You can chop up the leaves to make the process faster. Then, after eighteen months or so, you will have a beautiful bag of leaf mould to use in your garden in the same way you would regular garden compost.

What can I put in my compost?

Now this is the most important part of home composting; understanding what you can and cannot put into your compost bin. Compost needs a mix of carbon and nitrogen to work well. Too much nitrogen and your compost pile will become a slimy, smelly mess, or too much carbon and it will easily dry out, making it very tricky for the composting process to take place.

The easiest way to make sure you achieve a good balance in your compost heap is to think of your organic waste as two colours: green and brown. The green waste will provide the nitrogen and the carbon will come from the brown waste. I highly recommend separating out your green and brown waste, as this makes it easier to keep track of just how much is being added to your compost bin. There are so many different ideas around what the ratio of green to brown waste should be to make the best compost. Please do not get too caught up with this, ultimately you are making a big difference by just attempting to compost and these rules should not deter you. Over time you will figure out what ratio works best for you, but I like to aim for a mix of sixty per cent green waste and forty per cent brown waste. Try to avoid adding too much of any one material in one go, as this can upset the balance of your compost bin.

So just what is classed as green waste and what is classed as brown waste? I have made a little table below so you can have a quick reference guide, this is not a complete list as that would be hundreds of pages long, but it will give you a good idea of what you can use.

Green waste	Brown waste	What to avoid
Animal manure from animals with vegetable-based diets such as cows	Cardboard, shredded (avoid heavily coloured and plastic tape)	Cooked food
Annual weeds (not yet in seed)	Dead plant material (not diseased)	Dairy products
Coffee grounds	Egg boxes (cardboard only)	Diseased plant material
Green garden waste	Egg shells	Faeces, dog and cat
Leafy plants, soft	Newspaper, shredded	Fish
Leaves, fresh	Paper, shredded (avoid heavily coloured or embossed)	Meat
Seaweed and kelp	Pet bedding	Plants that have gone to seed
Tea bags (degradable only)	Plant stems, old	Oil and grease
Vegetable kitchen waste (uncooked)	Twigs and branches, small	Plastics
	Straw and hay, chopped up	Salt
	Woodchip, shredded	Too much of one type of waste

Top tips

* *To help speed up the composting process, chop up your ingredients into smaller chunks; this will create a larger surface area, allowing it to break down much faster.*
* *You can add acidic items such as citrus peels or pine needles but be careful not to add too many at once, as this will upset the balance of the compost pile, making it too acidic.*

Best practices and tips for compost success

Once you get your first batch of beautiful, crumbly, homemade compost, I promise you there will be no stopping you, and composting your organic waste will become second nature.

Occasionally your compost heap can run into a few issues, however. The good news is all of these issues are easily avoidable or simple to fix. Here are a few of my top tips to help you achieve compost success at home every time:

* Try to maintain a good balance of green and brown waste. Avoid adding too much of one component at a time, instead always try to add an equal mix.

* Quite a few of the problems your compost heap can encounter are caused by too much moisture from too much green waste. To dry out your compost heap, add a good amount of shredded paper or cardboard into the heap, and cover it to protect it from the rain for a few weeks to let it dry out.

* If your compost heap is quite dry, it is a good idea to add some water to it. You are aiming for a level of moisture where if you dig into the middle of the heap and squeeze it, a few drops of water should appear.

* Avoid composting seeds or diseased materials as the majority of compost heaps will not reach a high enough temperature to kill these. It is possible to compost these using hot composting, but I still prefer to not run the risk.

* While autumn leaves can be composted, they contain a lot of lignin, which causes them to break down more slowly than the rest of the heap. Autumn leaves are best bagged alone, and used to make leaf mould.

* Compost forms faster in warmer weather, so expect your compost to naturally slow down in the winter months.

Compost piles and keeping animals safe

Compost piles often make the perfect home for all sorts of wildlife in your gardens, from endangered hedgehogs and slow worms to mice, toads, bees and loads more. All of these animals have an important part to play in your garden ecosystem and should be protected.

I avoid using or disturbing my compost heap during the months where these animals are often hibernating. This is usually from October to March in my UK climate, and fortunately for me, I have very little need to disturb the pile during these months.

Compost piles often get a bad name for attracting vermin. I do not like this word vermin, as these animals often play a very important role in creating a balanced, self-sufficient garden. However, I completely understand if you wish to keep their presence in your garden to a minimum, especially if you have a smaller garden or balcony. Avoid adding cooked foods, or adding large amounts of kitchen waste at once and you will be absolutely fine.

For peat's sake, let's talk about peat!

Peat is, and has been for years, a key ingredient in the bagged compost you will find in the store. Peat seemed to be the perfect ingredient: it is cheap, easy to harvest, readily available and has all the qualities needed to make a brilliant compost mix. However, using peat has a dark side that has been ignored for all too long by big companies and governments. Only in the last few years has the impact of using peat really been widely publicised in the press.

Peat is a topic where us gardeners can really make a huge difference. The vast majority of peat taken from peatlands is extracted to be used in the horticultural industry. If we simply refuse to use it in our gardens, the incentives to extract it will fade, and hopefully this industry will cease to exist on the scale it does currently.

The peat used in these compost mixes is extracted from natural peatlands and bogs. This process really gets me going, so please forgive me if this turns into a bit of a rant! When I started writing this book, I promised myself that its purpose is to provide fun and exciting ways we can harness the power of our gardens, and use them for good, as well as help to tackle issues other people are ranting about. However, the use of peat in compost is so counterproductive and is essentially eco vandalism, and it is hard to not rant about it. Who knows, maybe someone might listen?

So, you may be asking, why is using peat such a problem? As we briefly touched on earlier, there are two main issues when it comes to destroying peatlands. The first issue is peatlands are complex and delicate ecosystems, with many plants and species found within them that are rarely found elsewhere. Sometimes the argument is put forward that peat is renewable, but unlike a tree, for example, which may take ten, twenty or even thirty years to regrow, peat can take hundreds or sometimes even thousands of years to form. It takes a bulldozer only a few minutes to rip out what has taken centuries to form and will take the same length of time to be replaced again.

The second issue is the detrimental impact it has on the planet. Peatlands have the ability to capture and store rotting plant material, in turn forming the peat and locking away lots of harmful carbon dioxide. Peatlands really are a fantastic weapon in our arsenal to combat global warming, and destroying them is not only counterproductive, but worsening the problem. To put into perspective just how effective peatlands are at carbon capture, they are currently storing more carbon dioxide than any form of vegetation, including all of the world's forests. When peatlands are drained and destroyed this carbon dioxide is released back into the atmosphere. To understand just how much carbon dioxide is stored in peatlands it is worth looking at the Indonesian forest fires in 2015. These peat swamp forest fires released sixteen million tonnes of carbon dioxide each day, which, to put it into perspective, is more than the entire USA was producing per day at that time!

Peat is not an irreplaceable ingredient in the bagged compost we buy in the stores, which makes this eco vandalism all that much worse. Sometimes in life there have to be environmental trade-offs, especially if something provides massive value and is irreplaceable. However, peat does not meet this criterion, as the damage caused far outweighs the reward gained.

So how can us gardeners help out? Luckily this is an easy one to fix. Simply try to avoid buying compost that contains peat. Making homemade compost is an obvious answer to this, but often you will need to supplement this with compost bought from the shops too. Peat-free compost is becoming widely available and has really improved since even just a few years ago. I have not used a peat-based compost in my garden for the last four years and everything is growing as well as, if not better than it ever has.

Top tip

Bagged compost marketed as 'organic' or 'reduced peat' will often not be peat free. Check the packaging and look for the words 'peat free', or 'zero peat'. Organic compost can be peat free, but it does not automatically mean so.

Good news story

England and Wales lead the way in banning peat sales to gardeners!

After years of debate, the sale of peat to gardeners will finally be banned in England and Wales from 2024. A ban for the wider horticultural industry will come into effect by 2030.

According to government estimates, once both bans are in place, this may cut carbon dioxide emissions by 4 million tonnes over the next couple of decades.

The horticultural industry combined with us gardeners are responsible for purchasing the majority of nearly all peat that is sold. So, by banning peat's main customer from purchasing it, hopefully this industry will start to slow right down.

This ban has forced companies to improve their range of peat-free compost mixes, and already far more peat-free alternatives are available to buy, in preparation for the ban.

Hopefully, England and Wales can lead the way in showing other countries around the world that peat is not an essential ingredient in our compost mixes.

The UK government have also released a plan to help fund restoration projects across the UK peatlands, with an aim of restoring 35,000 hectares by 2025.

Checklist

Have your notebook and pencil handy to make a note of your answers to the following prompts:

→ What food items do you often end up throwing away? Is there any way these can maybe be stored better or even preserved?

→ What has been your favourite method of preserving food so far?

→ Are there other methods of preserving you are yet to try, and if so, which one will you try next?

→ Have a think about if you have the space to start composting at home. If you do, which method is best suited for you?

→ Search for a good second-hand compost bin, or even consider making your own.

→ When purchasing compost, or even potted plants, try to check if the soil contains any peat. If it does, consider if there are any peat-free alternatives you can use.

4

Pop on your welly boots and grab an umbrella, we are collecting water

I debated long and hard about whether to include the topic of collecting and saving water in the garden within the last chapter, or to give it its own. As you can see, I have decided it needs its own stand-alone chapter as it is such an important topic. This is because water is the key to success in our gardens and outside spaces, so I believe it is important we learn how to make the most of this valuable resource.

In countries such as the UK we should have enough water to never be in need, but hosepipe bans are common nearly every summer. If you are reading this in a truly dry climate, such as parts of the USA and Australia, you may have a sarcastic smile on your face. While we get more than enough rain in the UK, our ability to store it is poor, and our ability to transport it is even worse. To illustrate quite how poor, In England and Wales we lose nearly three billion litres (around 660 million gallons) of water each day due to leaks and spillage.

Weather records will show we are getting the same amount of rainfall as we have for the last hundred years. Well, that may be true, but we need to look at how we are getting this rainfall. Big, heavy downpours of rain are becoming more common, and increasingly our winters are getting wetter and our summers are becoming drier. This poses two major problems. The first is that with the majority of rainfall coming in only a few months, it is very tricky to store as much water as if it was spread across the months of the year. Secondly, the demand for water is often much higher in the hotter drier summer months where the rainfall is becoming increasingly scarce. Demand in general is a lot higher now than it has been in the past. So, although the levels of rainfall may be the same, it needs to be stored in a better way, and also must meet the needs of far more people. Heaven forbid we get a dry winter, and we soon find ourselves in quite a bit of trouble.

The reason to collect water and manage its usage is pretty obvious in hot dry climates, however, due to these highlighted issues, we no longer have the luxury of not having to worry about this topic in the more traditionally wet climates, such as the UK. If we do not start to take this issue seriously, soon collecting and storing water will go from a choice to a necessity.

While most people who capture and store rainwater do so to water their plants, this is far from the only reason why you might want to. Not everything we use water for requires the use of heavily treated clean tap water. In fact, for many of these activities, using tap water is completely unnecessary and a bit of a waste. Activities such as washing cars, filling up ponds and fountains, building water features and mixing building materials are all great examples of where you can happily use rainwater captured in the garden instead.

Before continuing on with this chapter, please check your local laws. In the vast majority of countries and states, collecting rainwater is completely legal, and some local governments will even help you do this, as it is in their best interests to reduce dependency on mains water. However, some states in the USA, such as Colorado, Utah, Nevada, Illinois and Arkansas, have some regulations in place, to limit the collection of rainwater on your property. Some of the reasoning for these regulations is a little bit strange in my opinion, but that is not something we will explore here. However, for the vast majority of people reading this, you will be absolutely fine to start collecting that precious rainwater in your gardens.

Why is using a lot of mains tap water in the garden a problem?

Ultimately, fresh water has a finite supply, and treated mains tap water even more so. Using fresh water in our gardens to water our plants, fill up ponds and build structures can remove the availability of this clean water from other more important uses. Mains water, which is what the majority of our hose pipes use, has been treated at the expense of a lot of energy, to make sure it is of the highest quality. The water we use in our gardens often does not need to be such high quality, and in a lot of climates there are more than enough ways by which we can save untreated rainwater to use instead. There are a lot of good reasons why we should think about reducing our dependency on mains water, so many, in fact, it is impossible to cover them just one small chapter. However, I have selected a few key reasons to highlight, before we move on to the fun part of learning how to collect it:

FEWER RESERVOIRS

The reservoirs used to store our water are often made by submerging natural valleys, causing immense damage to wildlife and the destruction of ecosystems. As a result, the lower the demand for mains water the fewer reservoirs need to be built, and the fewer reservoirs that need to be made, the better!

REDUCE WATER EXTRACTED FROM ELSEWHERE

When these reservoirs run low, water is often drawn directly from other natural sources, such as lakes and rivers, often with very little regard of what that will do to the surrounding wildlife and ecosystem. When these reservoirs are running low, that is often when these natural sources are running low too! Often due to our greed, the wildlife that relies on them can be left with very little.

REDUCING ENERGY AND CHEMICAL USAGE

To make water safe for our consumption, it has to go through quite an intensive treatment, involving various different chemicals. This is a long process that uses a lot of energy, and once it is complete, even more energy is used to pump this water into our homes and gardens. Not only is it a shame to waste this energy, the cost of this process is passed on to us in our water bills. When you are using mains water in the garden, you are paying for this high-quality water that you simply do not need; it is a waste of not only that treated water but also of your hard-earned money.

USING WATER AT THE WORST TIME

Due to the nature of gardening, us gardeners are guilty of using a lot of water at the worse time possible. I will be the first to admit that having a beautiful garden requires a lot of water, especially during the summer months. Using stored rainwater is a fantastic way to supply your garden with the water it needs. However, most gardeners will use mains water from the hose instead, and will use collected rainwater from water butts, as a secondary method of watering.

MAINS WATER MAY EVEN BE BAD FOR YOUR PLANTS

Chances are if you are reading this book, the mains tap water where you live is very high quality. It is a waste to use this mains water on your plants, as they do not need water of this quality, and in many cases the treated water can even be detrimental to the plant's health. A lot of the minerals found in tap water, especially tap water in hard-water areas, can raise the pH of the soil around your plant's roots, affecting the availability of nutrients, and hampering plant growth and development.

Luckily, there are so many ways we can use our gardens, big and small, to help out. Many methods require very minimal financial outlay and are pretty easy to set up and use.

How to collect rainwater in your garden

The easiest way to reduce your dependency on mains tap water is to start collecting rainwater in your garden. Doing this does not need to be difficult, nor expensive. There are so many ways you can collect a substantial amount of water in the garden, and here are my favourites:

WATER BUTTS

Using water butts is by far the best, easiest and most effective way to collect large volumes of rainwater at home. Water butts are traditionally a plastic container, ranging from 100 to 1,000 litres (22 to 220 imperial gallons) and more. Many local councils will supply you with water butts for free, so it is always worth checking your local area, however, they are pretty cheap to buy in the stores and you can even find cheap second-hand ones too. You will need to connect gutters to all your outside roofs, such as from the house roof and from sheds, garages and greenhouses which will catch and collect large volumes of water runoff every time it rains. To store this water simply run a downpipe from the gutter into the water butt. I like to add a wire mesh at the top of the downpipe, to catch any debris running into the water. You will be surprised just how much water you will accumulate after

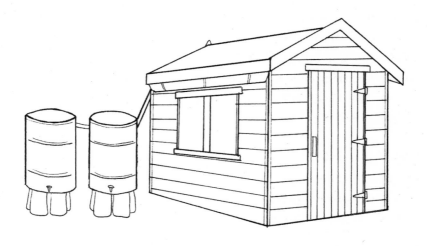

a heavy or prolonged rainfall. To avoid overflow, I highly recommend connecting two or three water butts together, so they can fill up in sequence, and no water is wasted due to overflow.

> **Top tip**
> *Most water butts will come with a small tap at the bottom to release the water. I highly recommend using a water butt with a very wide-opening top, which will easily allow you to fit your watering can into so you can fill it up that way. Filling up your watering can by using the small tap can be very slow, whereas dunking a watering can into the top is much faster, and trust me, this will halve the time it takes to water your garden.*

LARGE TROUGHS

At my allotment I have two large troughs, which I believe used to be water troughs for the cows from the farm behind us. If you have no outside structures in your garden where it is possible to connect guttering,you can collect a surprising amount of rainwater by simply placing some large open troughs around the garden. Troughs have the added benefit of allowing you to easily scoop out the water with your watering can, making them quick to use. During periods of hot dry weather, it is a good idea to cover the tops of your troughs, as this will help reduce evaporation and stop smaller animals and birds from falling in and drowning. Please make sure to include an escape route for any smaller animals that may fall in, a few old bricks, or rocks piled up by one side will be fine.

LARGE BUCKETS

If you do not have the space for large troughs, a similar outcome can be achieved by using large buckets. As with troughs, please add an escape route for anything that may fall in so it does not drown.

Later in this book we will explore the wonderful world of ponds, and all the fantastic benefits they can have for your garden. Having a pond in your garden can act almost as your own personal water reservoir. Every time it rains, as long as your pond is not under cover, it will naturally fill. This will allow you to collect even more water, which you can divert to other areas of your garden in times of need.

Important note

Collecting water is fantastic, but please remember to offer some for your local wildlife. It is important to cover your water butts, troughs and buckets to avoid evaporation and mosquitos laying their eggs. However, by doing this you are removing access to valuable water for your local wildlife. Take some of this collected water and leave it in small saucers around the garden for wildlife. It is wise to sprinkle some rocks in these saucers as well, to allow pollinating insects to safely drink too.

Be water wise in the garden

Collecting and storing water is only one side of the story. Learning how to use this water effectively is just as important to ensure we make the most of every single drop of this most valuable resource. Naturally us gardeners often have much higher levels of water consumption compared to the average person, and as a result we are possibly the group of people who waste the most water. I know I have certainly been guilty of this in the past!

Due to the natural timing of plant growth, often we need the most water for the garden at a time when it is most scarce, so it is important we take care of every drop. Luckily there are many very simple steps we can take to reduce our water usage in the garden, and here are my top tips for how we can be a little bit more water wise:

* Try using smaller watering cans, as they are far easier to use around the garden. Not only do they spill less water, but they are easier to aim, accurately delivering the water where you need it most.

* Where possible, it is important to try to use a watering can rather than a hose pipe. Firstly, as we have mentioned, often the water coming out of your hose is clean-treated mains water. This water is of a quality that is simply wasted on your plants, and can even hamper their growth. Secondly, when you use a hose pipe it is very easy to spray water all over the garden. This water will then evaporate and never offer any real benefit to your plants.

* When watering your crops, make sure you aim the water down to where the roots are. If you pour water all over the plant, a large amount of it will remain on the leaves, where it will evaporate.

* Give priority to your newly planted plants, as these will always require more water than plants that are already established. When established, plants can often go without water for quite a few days.

* In the second chapter of this book, we explored how using containers is a fantastic way to grow plants at home (see page 28). Containers are undoubtedly great, but try your best to use the largest containers possible, as these will require less frequent watering.

* Plant out your seedlings and small potted plants into the ground or larger pots as soon as possible. Due to the size of the small starter pots, they will often need watering two or three times a day!

* Use that fantastic garden gold compost we spoke about in the last chapter to mulch (add a layer) around your plants and lock in moisture.

* Weeds will appear in your garden no matter how hard you try to stop them. While you cannot prevent this from happening, you can control these weeds once they do appear. Try your best to remove as many weeds as possible, as they will create competition for moisture. It is worth noting this only applies to areas of the garden where you are growing crops or flowers that need to be watered.

* Let your lawns turn brown when it is dry! I understand this might not look the best, but I promise you, as soon as you get your next rainfall, they will bounce back and return to that lovely luscious green colour.

* Some plants are more drought tolerant than others, so consider this when planning your garden. Leafy greens such as lettuce can be quite water demanding, whereas crops such as carrots are more drought tolerant. Consider swapping out

some more water-intensive plants for drought-resistant ones, to save substantial amounts of water over the course of the growing season.

* If you are using pots to grow your plants, it is important they have drainage holes in the bottom, to prevent your plants from becoming waterlogged. To avoid this excess drained water going to waste, place a saucer underneath the pot to capture it. You can then pour this excess water onto your other plants.

* Some people need a way to automatically water their gardens, and for years the sprinkler system has filled this need. Sprinklers can be extremely wasteful. Instead, try to use a drip irrigation system, as they are better at delivering water to the plants roots, where it is usually needed most.

* Try to avoid watering during the heat of the middle of the day (unless you are saving a wilted plant). Instead, water in the mornings or the evenings, as this will help reduce evaporation, and allow your plants to absorb more moisture.

* When it comes to watering, giving your plants a big drink once every few days will always be more beneficial than a light daily sprinkle. Plus, a light daily sprinkle will often use more water as you will lose more to evaporation.

Top tip

You can create an automatic plant watering system by burying a terracotta pot into your soil, plugging the drainage hole with garden tack or white tack and then filling the pot up with water. The water will slowly seep out of the porous terracotta, going into the surrounding soil, right where the roots are. It is a good idea to pop a lid over this pot to reduce evaporation and prevent mosquitos from laying their eggs in the water.

Good news story

An Irish teenager has won an international science award for an ingenious method which can remove microplastics from our water.

I am sure by now many of us are aware of the terms microplastics and the massive damage these plastics are causing the environment. Well, could that all be about to change?

Fionn Ferreira from west Cork has been developing a method of removing microplastics from water, which in initial testing has proven to be 87% effective at removing plastic particles less than 5mm in diameter.

This groundbreaking project shines hope on what is fast becoming a massive global issue. Microplastics can come from a wide range of sources from soaps and facial scrubs to packaging. If these microplastics end up in our waterways this can prove very damaging to wildlife, especially fish, as the small plastic particles are accidentally mistaken for food! Once ingested by the smaller creatures, these microplastics can work their way up the food chain, eventually even affecting us humans.

Ferreira has been using ferrofluids, a combination of oil and magnetite powder, combined with magnets to help remove this nasty microplastic from the water.

While there is still some work to be done before this can be effectively used on an industrial scale, combined with many countries banning products containing microplastics, it is certainly an exciting step in the right direction!

Staying safe using stored water

Storing water has so many benefits, both for your garden and the environment as well as your wallet. But there are a few things to be careful of. Stored water is often not of the highest quality, and you need to handle and use it with a degree of caution. It should go without saying, please never drink it! Instead, focus on using it in the garden, for washing the car, using for building, washing the greenhouse, filling up ponds and watering your plants, but *never* for human or pet consumption.

The quality of stored water is not always the best, so here are a few tips to minimise risk and stay safe when using it:

* Keep your stored water in shade to reduce the growth of bacteria. The warmer the temperatures the easier it will be for bacteria to take over.

* Add a filter to your rain gutters to help avoid debris going into the storage system, which can often help to cause more bacterial growth. This filter does not have to be complicated; it can be as simple as a metal wire mesh attached to the downpipe.

* Always wash your hands after handling stored water. Good hand hygiene after being in the garden in general is always a good idea. I keep a tub of hand sanitiser in my garden shed, as a reminder to use it, then I always wash my hands upon returning indoors.

* Clean your water butts at least once a year, to avoid a build up of slime and bacteria. During a time in the year when your water butt is empty, remove it from the guttering system, and clear out any debris that has accumulated in the bottom.

* It is a good idea to disconnect your hose pipes when you are not using them, to avoid water sitting in the pipes for long periods of time. Water sat in hose pipes can harbour quite a few nasty bacteria, as well as get hot enough to burn you (or your plants) in the summer sun.

Flooding

An added incentive to capture and store rainwater at home, is its possible ability to reduce the flood risk in your garden. Flooding is often caused by excess water run-off, which recently has been a lot more common, due to more frequent heavy downpours of rain. A good guttering system on the roof of any outside buildings connected to a water butt can significantly reduce the effects of surface water run-off, and in turn can reduce the effects of flooding. Before I connected guttering and water butts to my shed, garage and greenhouse, the surrounding areas would always flood after heavy rainfall. This water would then often run throughout the garden, saturating the soil, leading to further flooding. Along with planting trees (which we will discuss later, see page 220), collecting and storing water has been the most effective way by which I have managed to reduce flood risks in the garden.

Checklist

Have your notebook and pencil handy to make a note of your answers to the following prompts:

→ What methods of water capture are you using in your garden?

→ What is your primary method of watering the garden? Are you using a hose pipe or watering can?

→ Have you connected guttering to your outside roofs?

→ Do you have water butts connected to your garden guttering?

→ Will your watering can fit into the top of your water butt?

→ Is your stored water covered over to reduce the effects of evaporation?

→ Are you keeping your stored water in the shade to reduce bacterial growth?

→ Have you considered planting more drought-resistant plants?

Upcycling in the garden and the P-word, plastic!

You may or may not be aware of the term upcycling. I would just like to quickly clarify what my personal take on this term is, and how I will use it throughout this chapter. I use the term upcycling to refer to the process of taking an item that is destined for the recycling or even the bin, and repurposing it in a creative way to give it another purpose. This in turn will help keep it away from landfill, while also saving you a little bit of money.

I like to think of the number of people who could benefit from upcycling to realize its true potential. It is predicted that as many as fifty-five per cent of American households participate in gardening, which when expressed as a number is well over one hundred and fifty million people, and that is just America alone! Add the UK and Europe to this and that number nearly doubles. And that is before we even think about Asia, Africa and beyond. Long story short, there are a lot of us gardeners out there. The way I like to think about upcycling is if all gardeners just swapped out buying twenty or thirty things a year (which is actually very easy to do) and instead replaced them with an upcycled alternative, that could save more than four billion – yes, billion, with a b – pieces of rubbish being thrown away, and ending up who knows where. On top of that, it will also prevent four billion other items being manufactured, and all of the packaging waste that comes along with that.

I love upcycling. Not just for the environmental help it offers, but also because it allows me to reconnect with a childhood love of arts and crafts, while saving money at the same time. You can upcycle all sorts of things, for all sorts of uses, but for me the one hobby that utilizes upcycling the best is gardening. Yes, I may be biased, but let me explain why this makes sense. In your home, you want everything to be aesthetically pleasing. Let's be honest, unless you are a master craftsman, you can tell when something is upcycled. With gardening, you are often upcycling for a purpose, not for the look of the thing. As long as it is functional, who cares if your watering can is an old milk bottle, or your plant labels are used lolly sticks?

To explain why upcycling is potentially becoming a more important life skill and not just a hobby, I would like to tell a very quick story.

As a child I was lucky enough to be given a collection of Victorian gardening tools from my grandparents. Amazingly, some of these tools are more than 150 years old! Surprisingly, other than the odd repair here and there, overall they are as good as new.

These tools live a hard life, being used practically every day, often to do jobs they are not designed to do. In more than twenty years of personally using them, I am yet to break one. Thinking about it, I have not even really badly damaged one either. These tools were handmade in the UK, and probably were very expensive when they were new. However, while they may have been expensive, we have certainly got our money's worth. I am now the third generation of my family using them, and there was even a family using them before mine!

Obviously new tools have come out over the years, and being slightly addicted to all things gardening, I more often than not buy them. However, I am yet to find a single tool, including many built by the 'premium' brands, that even come close to my Victorian set. Cheap plastic handles are everywhere, and often snap at the first sign of intense stress, metal bends or snaps the minute it hits anything of substance, and do not get me started on the completely over-the-top level of packaging you are forced to purchase if you want the tool!

This got me thinking, and the longer I thought about it, the more I realized this pattern is seen across nearly all products, not just my gardening tools. Unfortunately, these days it seems to be getting harder and harder to find products that are built to last.

However, while creating the waste can be quite hard to avoid these days, throwing it away is our choice, and that is where our good old friend the garden comes in to help us. By thinking creatively, we can use our gardens, no matter the size, as our very own recycling plant. Now, I am not saying we can use and repurpose every bit of waste we create, obviously that is virtually impossible. But collectively if we all save a few bits here and there, it will make such a big change, plus as you will soon find out, save you a lot of money, as well as saving more waste from entering the cycle.

What is slightly ironic is us gardeners as a collective are often guilty of creating a lot of waste, especially plastic. As a dedicated bunch, we buy a lot for our hobby and nearly everything we use in the garden comes in plastic packaging or plastic containers or the product itself is made from plastic. It has been estimated that there are over five hundred million plastic plant pots in circulation, which is just one example of many I could have highlighted. However, we don't have to be part of this problem: by using some of the tips and tricks we talk about in this chapter we can dramatically reduce our own plastic footprint. Hopefully this chapter will inspire your own creativity and you will come up with your own amazing ways to upcycle in your gardens and outside spaces.

The plastic problem

No type of waste is great, but one captures all the headlines, and rightfully so. By now we all know there is a global issue with the level of plastic we use and throw away. Highlighting the problems of plastic is important, but I refuse to join the club of people focusing on how doomed we all are, as to be honest that is the last thing we need right now! I would instead like to show just how effective we can be at reducing this plastic waste in our gardens, and to offer a few solutions to this problem, many of which are very easy to do and to implement.

Are we drowning in plastic?

If you think about it, plastic is everywhere; nearly everything we buy either contains plastic or is packaged in plastic. The production methods used to make the plastic are not great for the environment. However, the bigger problem with plastic is just how long it will remain on our planet and in our ecosystems after it is made, and just what we do about this.

In my research for this chapter, I decided to have a look at my own garden and take a plastic audit – the results really shocked me! Nearly everything I use in the garden contains plastic! Water butts, pots, labels, feed containers, compost bags, tool handles, watering cans, polytunnels, bins, wire coating, nets, weed barriers, gloves, cane toppers and plant supports. I mean, I could easily keep going but I think you get the picture.

During this audit I noticed some plastics are obvious, like plastic pots, whereas others are quite sneaky and not so obvious, such as horticultural fleece and wire coating. There were also a wide range of plastics being used too!

The common plastics I found in the garden are:

Plastic type	Common use	Issues
PVC (Polyvinylchloride)	Tools and water pipes	Extreme heat may cause chemical leaching
LDPE (Low–density polyethylene)	Compost and raw material bags	Not particularly easy to recycle
PP (Polypropylene)	Pots, trays, twine and netting	If coloured black it is very hard to recycle.

I would just like to add, while gardening can cause a lot of plastic waste, with a few simple changes that we will soon explore, your garden can have the reverse effect and help reduce a considerable amount of plastic waste.

What are the problems with all this plastic?

It is important we realize and understand the issues surrounding the use and disposal of plastic, as it will impact us all. But having said that, I would like to keep this brief, as focusing on the solution is far more effective than focusing on the problem.

So, just why is plastic such a problem?

DEGRADES SLOWLY

Due to the chemical structure of plastic, it is often very slow to degrade, with some types of plastic taking hundreds and hundreds of years to break down, often leaving microplastics and other contaminants.

VARIABLE RECYCLING CAPABILITIES

Unlike some materials, such as glass, it is hard to recycle plastic over and over again, as it will degrade a little each time. Recycling is fantastic, but for plastics it is not an effective long-term solution. Quite a few plastics currently are hard to recycle as the technology is not quite there, provisions vary massively with geography and these recycling techniques can be very energy intensive. There can also be issues with contamination, as the plastic needs to be thoroughly cleaned before it can be recycled.

PLASTIC WASTE IN OCEANS

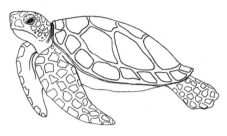

Unfortunately, a lot of plastic waste will end up in our oceans. It is estimated that nearly eight million tonnes of plastic a year finds its way into our oceans, causing immense damage to the wildlife that calls them home. By now I am pretty sure we have all seen the upsetting images of the destruction this causes.

COST

Plastic is relatively cheap to mass produce compared to other alternatives, which has for years made it a popular choice in manufacturing. In the UK alone over five million tonnes of plastic are consumed each year, and in the USA it is estimated this number is anywhere between forty and fifty million metric tonnes, which has led to plastic becoming one of the most common forms of waste.

Important note

While some types of plastic are not yet widely available for home recycling, many garden centres and supermarkets offer more specialized means of recycling. You can often drop off plastics such as old compost bags at your local garden centre.

How can you help reduce the use of plastics in the garden?

Gardening, and more importantly gardeners, seem to be leading the way when it comes to dealing with this issue. In general, us gardeners are a pretty eco-conscious bunch, and for good reason – gardens are reliant on external factors such as wildlife and weather for success. So it is in our best interests to do our bit and make sure we look after the natural world, which provides us with so much.

The good news is that being such an eco-conscious bunch has forced horticultural companies to become a bit more eco conscious too. This means it is not too tricky to make a few adjustments here and there to dramatically reduce our plastic consumption for gardening, compared to many other hobbies and interests.

Now I mentioned earlier that I have lots of plastic in my garden, and I would bet many others do too. However, I do have a good excuse! Nearly everything I have in my garden that is plastic, I have inherited over the years from other people. My plastic pots are older than me, the watering cans are from when I was a child, and I have been getting tangled in the same plastic netting for the last twenty years! This is not just an excuse, but quite an important message. If you are just getting into gardening, then you have the ability to look for good plastic alternatives, but if like me you already have a lot, it is as important to look after it and avoid disposing of it.

Here are a few of my top tips to help reduce the amount of plastic used in the garden:

* Where possible try to buy in bulk. Great examples are compost, wood chips or garden stones. If you already use a lot of compost, or if you plan to start growing your own food at home, you will need a lot and ordering one bulk bag will use far less packaging than buying lots of smaller individual bags. Plus, you will often save quite a bit of money too.

*   Better still, start making compost at home. As we saw earlier, by making compost at home, you can help reduce the amount of plastic compost bags you buy.

*   Try to buy products that have minimal plastic packaging. Look to see if there is a plastic-free packaging version of whatever it is that you are buying.

*   When growing plants at home, try to plant direct and skip out the need for plastic seed-starting trays and plastic pots.

*   If you look after your plastic it can last a very long time, helping to avoid throwing it away. Keep your plastic out of direct sunlight, as that can make it brittle, and give it a good wash at the end of each growing season.

*   Try to buy non-plastic alternatives. A great example is wooden handles instead of plastic on your tools.

*   Think about what you can upcycle and use in your garden (later in this chapter we will look at some really cool upcycling examples you may want to use).

*   Propagate as many plants as you can to save on packaging. Try taking a cutting of mint or basil and popping it in water. It will grow roots and you can grow it on, avoiding having to buy a new plant and all the packaging that comes with it.

Nature has so many natural ways to make what you are buying. A great example of this is to swap out liquid plant food, which is often sold in plastic containers, for homemade stinging nettle feed.

How to make stinging nettle plant food

Making nettle tea plant food is a fantastic way to give your plants a boost, while also reducing plastic containers from shop-bought plant foods.

* To make stinging nettle plant food, simply chop up a good number of stinging nettles into a deep, watertight container such as a metal bucket.

* Add some rainwater to this container, making sure the nettles are completely submerged. I like to use a brick to weigh them down. (Tap water will work too, but rainwater is always best.)

* Place this bucket of nettles out in the garden, and leave for three weeks to ferment and rot down. Just a word of caution, this can get a bit smelly so keep it as far away as possible.

* After around three or four weeks your nettle tea mixture will be ready! This nettle tea will be packed full of nitrogen and other nutrients your plants will adore.

* The raw nettle tea will be too concentrated to give straight to your plants. Instead dilute it one part nettle tea to ten parts water. This can then be added straight to your plant's roots, once every two weeks.

* As you have probably gathered by now, I have a lot of plants. One 15 litre (3 gallon) metal bucket of nettle tea will often last me all through the main growing season, helping me to avoid buying liquid feed in plastic bottles.

Plastic alternatives to use in the garden

Reducing, recycling and looking after the plastic we already have are all important steps we can take to help out, but ultimately the best course of action is to look for alternatives to plastic. Luckily for us gardeners, we are spoilt for choice. As mentioned before, we are typically a pretty eco-conscious bunch, so the companies selling to us have to be as well. It just goes to show, ultimately it is the consumer who controls how eco friendly a sector is.

Now let's not forget, there are environmental costs to everything and unfortunately when making a purchase, it is often a case of choosing the least-damaging option. My top recommendation would be to use as many tips as you can from the next section, where we look at what you can upcycle to put to use in the garden (see page 138). That way you will save yourself a little bit of money, as well as stop a little bit of waste being added to the growing pile in landfill.

So here are my top plastic alternatives to look for:

BAMBOO

There are so many great companies replacing plastics with bamboo. The great part about using bamboo is just how fast it grows, making it a great substitute for plastic. I have quite a few bamboo pots, dibbers and tools, and for the most part they have held up pretty well when put through their paces in the garden. The negative with bamboo is that bamboo equipment is still quite expensive, usually costing two or three times what a plastic equivalent will cost.

Bamboo is great for, pots, seed trays, hand tools, dibbers, plant labels, gloves and plant supports.

WOOD

Wood is a great material for a lot of uses in the garden, and it is even better if it is reclaimed, such as old pallet wood. When using wood, it is important to check that it is ethically sourced and as sustainable as possible. Quite a lot of my older gardening supplies have wooden components, and with a bit of care they are still going strong! Wooden equipment will require a little bit more care than plastic, but this will soon become second nature.

Wood is great for hand tools, small tool handles, large tool handles, plant supports, large pots, containers, seed trays, plant labels and raised beds.

Important Note

Wood will often need to be treated in order to be used successfully in the garden. While there are many ways this can be achieved, I would avoid using creosote. Not only is it not great for the environment, it is especially undesirable near plants you are growing to eat as it is potentially harmful for your health. In many countries the sale of creosote is banned, but in countries where this is not the case, there are many other safer substitutes you can use.

METAL

Well looked-after, high-quality metal really will last a lifetime. This is what really sets it apart from the rest of the materials mentioned. I have quite a few metal watering cans, troughs and tools, many of which are well over a hundred years old. Metal will usually be the most expensive alternative, with the initial outlay often being quite a few times higher than plastic. However, over a lifetime it will most likely work out to be the most economical as you only need to buy it once. Just be careful of cheap metals. They will more often than not be brittle and not fit for purpose, as I have found out the hard way.

Metal is great for many different garden tools and equipment, but there is one thing I would not recommend it for, and that is pots. This is due to the fact that in the summer metal pots will reach unbearable temperatures, and vice versa in the winter, making life for plants in metal pots very tricky indeed.

NATURAL FIBRES

This is one of my favourite plastic replacements, as many of the natural fibres used are waste products, often destined for landfill. Using it is essentially a whole industry upcycling on a mass scale, which is fantastic. There are a range of fibres being used at the moment, but the most popular one is coco coir. This is upcycled into all sorts of cool things for your garden, some are obvious, such as string, others not so much, such as expanding compost.

Natural fibres are great for pots, string, outside mats, netting and gloves.

GLASS

Glass is great for plant cover and plant protection. Other than plastic, glass is one of the only transparent materials, which makes it so valuable in the garden, as this is essential for plant growth. Glass can be delicate, and yes, I have broken my fair share, but as long as you are careful it is a fantastic material. The glass on my big greenhouse is over thirty years old. It is cleaned every winter and looks as good as new. If I compare this to the plastic cover over my polytunnel, which tends to last only five or six years, and that is providing the wind doesn't get to it first; glass is a far better investment.

However, please do not read this and start replacing your plastic watering can for a metal one, and swapping that old netting for a natural fibre blend one instead. If you already have plastic tools and equipment, simply look after them and get as much life from them as possible. Then once it finally gives out, think if you can upcycle it, and if not, can you recycle it? Then at this stage it is worth looking buying a plastic-free alternative, ideally one where you will get a lot of usage from it.

Upcycling in the garden

I owe a lot to upcycling. In the early days of my online social media journey, the videos that built the majority of my audience were videos around upcycling waste in the garden. Ultimately this audience is what led to me getting the opportunity to write this book, so from me, upcycling gets a big thumbs up!

Sometimes people think of upcycling as just repurposing old plastic bottles and newspapers; and yes, that is part of it, but it can be so much more than that! I have upcycled pallets and reclaimed wood into all sorts of fun things, as you are about to see, many of which can save you a lot of money! Writing this chapter got me thinking about what I have upcycled in my own garden, and I thought it would be fun to see how much money I have saved. Put simply, the answer was massive – around £12,000 in fact!

> **Top tip**
> *When upcycling you can often use multiple components to create a bigger, more effective project. A great example of this is my raised bed/cold frame. I used old reclaimed wood to make a raised bed structure, then used old compost bags to line it, and placed an old window on top to turn it into a cold frame in the winter. The total cost for me was zero, but to buy a cold frame of this size would cost well over £200!*

Now obviously that was not all from turning plastic bottles into watering cans. The bulk of that money came from my larger-scale DIY projects. I have used old pallets and reclaimed wood to make a lot of otherwise quite expensive furniture, as well as old windows and glass to make cold frames, and old farmyard troughs to make water butts. And don't get me started on how much money I save by making my own compost, and yes, even the compost bins to make this compost are upcycled! The fact that I garden on an almost industrial scale means I need a lot of equipment, and this has all combined to make up that £12,000 saving.

The upcycling tricks I recommend for every garden

It is time to have some fun and have a look at what we repurpose and upcycle. Below are a few examples of my most common and favourite things to upcycle, but this is by no means a complete list. Once you get started, you will get the creative juices flowing, and before long you will be creating your very own upcycling projects.

PLASTIC MILK/JUICE BOTTLE WATERING CAN

Take an empty milk or juice bottle and remove any labels. Wash out any residue and remove the cap. Poke five or six holes into the cap. I like to use a sharp nail, but a fork that has been heated over a flame works well too. Also poke one hole in the top of the handle. Fill this bottle back up with water and you now have a upcycled watering can that works really well, especially for seedlings.

YOGHURT SEED-STARTING POTS

Wash out your empty yoghurt pots and poke a few holes in the bottom for drainage. Try to keep a few different sizes for different sizes of seeds. These yoghurt pots make fantastic seed-starting pots and can be used for years!

NEWSPAPER SEED-STARTING POTS

Newspapers make the perfect eco seed-starting pots. All you need to do is rip out a page and fold it in half. Pop a jar at one end and roll the newspaper into a cylinder. Push the jar down to compress the bottom, then remove the jar. These brilliant little eco-friendly pots can just be planted out whole once the seedling is big enough, and they will just break down into the soil.

TOILET ROLL SEED-STARTING POTS

If you do not have access to newspapers, toilet roll or kitchen roll tubes also make fantastic seed-starting pots. All you need to do is chop the roll into 10 cm (4 in) deep cylinders and pop these into an old fruit punnet. Just like newspapers, you can plant out the whole tube into the soil, which is especially helpful for crops with tender roots such as peas and turnips.

PLASTIC BOTTLE CLOCHE

Large plastic bottles make amazing cloches. Cut the bottoms off these and keep them to be used as seed trays. Place the rest of a water bottle over one of your plants and this will act as a cloche, helping to protect against frost. I like to remove the bottle cap and poke a cane through the opening down into the soil. This will stop the bottle cloche from blowing away in the wind. Cloches will also help offer some protection from wildlife, but please be aware that a very determined animal will often find a way to remove the cloche, which is why I use them more for weather protection than wildlife protection.

OLD PLASTIC COOKIE/FRUIT PUNNET PROPAGATOR

Fruits and cookies mainly come in plastic punnets, often with a closing lid. Remove any labels and poke some holes in the bottom. When filled with compost these make the perfect seed-starting trays, and you can close the lid to create a mini propagator to help speed up seed germination.

LOLLY STICK PLANT LABELS

When you finish with your ice creams or lollies, if they have wooden sticks, rinse them off as they can be used as plant labels. If you write on them with pencil, you can easily rub this off at the end of the growing season and re-use it next year.

EGG CARTON SEED TRAY

Cardboard egg boxes make the perfect seed trays! They have ready-made spacing for each seed, which will help keep the roots separated from one another. Once your seedlings are ready to be planted out, a spoon will perfectly scoop out the root ball from each egg hole.

COMPOST BAG LINER

Empty compost bags are so useful, but my favourite way to use them is as liners for hanging baskets and raised beds. Poke a few holes in the bag and use it to line your hanging baskets. This will help slow down the rate at which water drains from your baskets, and will reduce the amount you need to water.

PALLET HERB PLANTER

Old wooden pallets are my favourite thing to upcycle, and making pallet planters is a brilliant way to use them. Turn your pallet so the wooden planks are horizontal, and remove every other plank to create a space between each one. Nail or staple large empty compost bags to the front and back planks to create a sort of hammock. Poke holes into these hammocks and then fill them up with compost, giving you often six or eight planting spaces in a small vertical planter. You can use these to plant strawberries, herbs and small flowers.

PALLET RAISED BED

Those planks that you removed from the pallets can be screwed or nailed together with a little bit of carpentry skill to create raised beds. Nearly all of the raised beds in my garden have been made this way and work great! You can even use old compost bags with holes poked in them for drainage as liners.

OLD SINK/BATH PLANTER

When we had our bathroom remodelled, I kept the sink and bath tub as these both have natural drainage, making them perfect for planters. When planted up with beautiful wildflowers they are stunning.

FARMYARD TROUGH WATER BUTT

My house is surrounded by farms, which often give away lots of cool things to upcycle. Old cow water troughs make the best water butts. Not only do they look cool, they hold a lot of water and are big enough to dip your whole watering can into, which really speeds up the rate at which you can water your garden.

OLD WELLIES FLOWER PLANTER

Wellington boots are a must in the garden, but eventually they will need to be replaced. Instead of throwing the old ones away, fill them with compost and plant your favourite flowers in the top.

GLASS JAR HANGING STORAGE

Old glass jars make brilliant watertight storage pods. Remove the lids and using short screws, screw the lid to the underside of wooden shelves. Once the jar lid is secured, you can screw and unscrew the glass jar to this, creating a hanging watertight storage system under your wooden shelves.

OLD CLOTHES SCARECROW

Later in this book we show you how to build a scarecrow (see page 217), and using your old clothes is a fantastic way to bring them to life as your garden friend.

TAKEAWAY CONTAINER TO GROW MICRO GREENS

Many food takeaways use little plastic or foil containers to package the food. If you add a thin layer of compost, sprinkle over some micro green seeds such as radish, then water and place another tray on top to create a little bit of weight to force the seeds to have contact with the growing medium, you can grow your own micro greens on your windowsill. Harvest your micro green tops with a sharp knife or scissors when they are around 6 cm (2½ in) tall.

COMPOST BAG BIN

Compost bags are pretty tough, so they make for the perfect storage bags or bin bags for garden waste that cannot be composted. I like to keep items such as wood chips and damaged terracotta pots in my old compost bags, and then store these until I need them.

TIN CAN VERTICAL PLANTER

Peel off the labels from your tin cans (the bigger the can the better) and paint them white (this will help stop them from getting too hot). Poke a few holes in the bottom and screw them hole-end down to a fence panel, wooden shed or any other wooden structure in the garden. Screw the tins positioned directly underneath one another, allowing space for the plants to poke out of the top, and this will create a self-watering system; as you water the top tins, the water will drain out of the drainage holes in the bottom and it will trickle down into the one below. Fill these tins with compost and plant out small plants such as lettuce or strawberries to create a fantastic vertical planter.

I hope this has given you a few ideas you might be able to transfer to your own garden, as well as sparking your imagination to create your own ways to upcycle in the garden.

Plastic-eating enzymes could be about to come to our rescue!

Enzymes that have the ability to break down plastic are nothing new. We have been exploring this potential technology for a few years now, but with relatively little success. However, a team at the University of Texas might be about to change that! With a little help from the power of AI, they have developed a new variant, which has the potential to break down plastics in as little as twenty-four hours.

This new enzyme, called hydrolase, can break down PET (polyethylene terephthalate) plastics into a molecular level, where it can then be recycled.

PET is one of the most common types of plastic, being primarily used in food and drink packaging. At early testing, hydrolase seems to be able to successfully break down mixed colour PET as well as clear. It is proving to be a pretty tough enzyme that, crucially, unlike many other plastic-eating enzymes in the past, seems to work outside of lab conditions.

Can our use of enzymes help create a circular plastics process? Well, the signs are certainly looking good!

Checklist

Have your notebook and pencil handy to make a note of your answers to the following prompts:

→ Carry out your own plastic audit in the garden and see just how much you can find.

→ Create a list of everything you need for the garden and try to list some plastic alternatives.

→ Make a note of what you have upcycled this week.

→ Decide on your favourite thing to upcycle so far.

→ Decide on the next upcycling project you would like to try.

→ List everything you have upcycled and work out how much money you have saved.

6

Furry friends and insect helpers

A few years ago, during a barbecue in my garden, a friend of mine commented on just how loud my garden is. He is right: birds are usually chirping; insects are buzzing around and leaves are rustling as who knows what scurries through. But you see, to me, this noise is a musical chorus of success. Not my success, but rather nature's. It is resilient for organisms to find a way to survive in a rapidly changing world. I have only played a very small part in this process, by simply allowing them to thrive.

For years, gardeners strived to control their gardens. As if almost trying to assert their dominance over Mother Nature. Unfortunately, the main weapons deployed to do so were various chemicals and pesticides. A few months ago, I was visiting an old manor house and garden and happened to find a very old advert from a newspaper cutting. This cutting was advertising a head gardener job. In big bold letters under the job description were the words, 'must be competent in the use of chemicals'. Unfortunately, I could not see the date from the advert. It is worth noting, though, that the use of chemicals has been documented as far back as 3,000 years ago, when they used sulphur compounds on their crops to help deter insects and bugs. The widespread use of chemicals this advert is referring to is most likely around the time of the Second World War. For years that is how things were done, obviously not by all gardeners at that time, but by enough to cause some damage. A garden's purpose for many was to look pretty, and possibly provide some food. The vast majority of the gardening literature from that time deemed any creature who dared to enter and potentially cause damage, public enemy number one! As a result, there was an extensive range of products on offer which were very effective at removing these 'pests', in fact maybe just a little bit too effective, and surprisingly some of these were actually still around and being used until only a few years ago. Garden creatures have sometimes been met with a barrage of chemical warfare, which gave them little to no hope of survival. However, in doing so there seemed to be no foresight, or possibly care, into any collateral damage, of which there was plenty.

Times are changing and with better and more information about the consequences, mainstream attitudes towards nature are too. One of the most satisfying parts of gardening, for me, is being able to engage with, and spot local wildlife, especially rare or endangered wildlife. I have been gardening for my whole life and it still excites me. I, like many others have watched documentaries by Sir David Attenborough, marvel in awe at these fantastic creatures. Happily, just a few feet away from the TV screen there is an equally amazing and intricate natural world outside in our gardens.

I can never stop myself from snapping a picture of any wildlife that comes into my garden. My phone is packed full of images of various frogs, toads, mice, birds, butterflies, bees, beetles, snakes, slowworms, newts, foxes, deer, badgers, hedgehogs and so much more. Each individual creature plays a small, but important, part in my small garden eco system. Other than some of the nearby farms (many of whom continue to nuke every creature who enters their land), I live in a pretty urban area. As a result, I view every animal who decides to call my garden home as a welcome friend. But this is by no means a one-way relationship. I help them, and as you shall see, they help me.

Stepping outside and hearing nature's hustle and bustle is just fantastic. This sound never fails to put a smile on my face. I like to think of it almost as if it is a busy factory floor, where all the factory workers have a small but very important job to do. Collectively they keep the factory running smoothly. The more factory workers there are, and the more diverse these workers are, the better the factory will run. What is our role in the factory? Well, in all honesty, I believe it is to give them the tools to do their job, and then sit back and enjoy the process, with minimal interference. And please, whatever you do, avoid using the nuclear option of pesticides on these humble garden workers, as you might soon find yourself short staffed!

It will take a long time to heal the damage done by our actions in the past. We are far from finished, but the good news is we are getting there. If we all chip in and start to slowly rebuild our little garden factories, nature will have a way to not only survive, but thrive! After all, we are sharing a small patch of outside land, so we may as well learn to all get along. The good, the annoying and even the slimy, as it really is in every creature's best interest that we coexist peacefully.

Inviting all of this wildlife to come and share the garden really is easy. We have all seen the films where the Disney princess opens the window and wildlife flocks in. Well, due to the habitat loss and unprecedented levels of urbanization, with a few very small additions or changes to your garden, wildlife will soon come streaming in. If you build it, I promise you they will come, and once they come, everything improves. Both in regards to the garden as well as your enjoyment of the garden.

Wildlife and the garden lifeline

Since the year 2000, the population of the UK has grown by more than 7 million people, and many other countries are experiencing a steady population growth too. Towns and cities are naturally growing to accommodate expanding populations. Unfortunately, this often comes at a cost to local wildlife, as we take their homes to build ours. Luckily modern housing developments are starting to incorporate plans for more green space and environmental areas, which is promising to see. But we have still built a rather fragmented environment for our wildlife to live in, as towns and cities start to divide up the natural landscape. This has meant many animals have had to learn to adapt, and those that cannot, will unfortunately start to disappear.

However, there is an easy way for us to help prevent that from happening. By simply using our gardens in a way where we can make space for what has been destroyed, we can dramatically lessen the impact of urbanization on wildlife.

This expansion of the human world, combined with a reduction in natural habitats, is forcing humans and animals to come into closer contact. In the last three years I have spotted more wildlife in my garden than ever before. Now I would love to claim this is all down to my ability to connect with nature and the fantastic rewilding job I have done. However, I suspect it has more to do with the twenty thousand new houses they have built in the surrounding areas.

One of my friends has purchased one of these new-build houses, and recently asked me how to deal with the deer that keep coming into the garden. But you see, only four years ago, that garden used to be a thriving woodland, which those same deer most likely called home. I had to gently remind him that his home was built on top of theirs.

Urbanization is not all bad, and a great example of how us humans coming together to help nature is birds. In the UK it is estimated that up to fifty per cent of people feed the birds in their gardens. As a result, many types of small garden bird are now thriving, in more numbers than ever before. While it would be better if these birds were thriving due to a natural cause, rather than a man-made intervention, the most important part is it shows what we can achieve when people start to care about wildlife. If we can pull together and accomplish this in a more natural way, such as planting more flowers, and leaving those flower heads to go to seed to provide food for the birds, and also for more different species, then we truly will make a massive difference.

It is for this reason, now more than ever, us gardeners need to lead the way in restoring some of nature's lost balance. Luckily, as we are about to explore, there are so many ways we can do this. As an added bonus, by doing so we are actually enhancing our own garden experience too.

Is it time to rephrase the word pest?

I despise the word pest. I always have done, and I always will do! Surely, there is no place in the world of gardening for a word that creates such bias and hatred, much of which is completely unjustified. Even as a child I freed animals from traps that had been set to control these so-called pests. Back then I did this because I used to think 'What if they have a family!', whereas now, it is more to do with an understanding of the balance of nature.

Humans have a habit of putting animals into a hierarchy of importance based on a certain level of cuteness. If they meet a certain standard, they have a right to life, and if not, well they are fair game to be eliminated. I can promise you our old friends Peter Rabbit and Bambi are capable of causing far more damage to our gardens than any slug ever will. In fact, very few slugs eat our precious plants. The vast majority feed off rotting plant matter and a range other thing including each other! However, they are labelled as a pest and therefore banned from our gardens and villainized. Meanwhile Mr and Mrs Rabbit are on the whole labelled as cute, and adored. Why is that? Well, I assume it all links back to our hierarchy of importance, based on how cute we deem an animal to be.

The problem is once a creature is labelled as a pest, it is deemed as bad or problematic, and immediately sentenced to death, especially if comes anywhere near our garden, and more animals are being forced into our gardens through no fault of their own. This continued usage of the word pest will simply send more innocent creatures to the executioner's block.

The ironic part is for our favourites to survive, we often need these so-called 'pests'. A UK favourite is hedgehogs, and I will admit I have a soft spot for them too. We even once took on some local rescue hedgehogs, which was a fantastic experience, and I am pretty sure their offspring still call the garden home today! However, if we wage war against 'pests' we are inadvertently waging war on hedgehogs and other favourites too, as they rely on slugs and other 'pests' for their food. Someone I know (who will remain nameless), uses slug pellets in the garden, and then in the same garden puts artificial food out for the hedgehogs. While their intentions are good, the irony still makes me chuckle.

Instead of thinking of certain creatures as pests, I like to think of them as being slightly more annoying than others. This removes the immediate want to eliminate them. For example, if you have multiple dogs, or any pets for that matter, I would place a bet that one is more annoying than the other. Garden creatures are no different. You seek to fix an annoyance; you don't seek to destroy it completely.

Your organic garden ecosystem

I get asked nearly every day on social media, what is the best way to control pests? My answer is simple: don't look to control, instead seek to let nature find its balance. This is rarely the answer people want to hear, as it is not an overnight fix. For me the best gardens are not the ones with the prettiest flowers, the biggest vegetable patch, or the most impressive lawn. But rather the most well-balanced garden, where every living creature, including us, is coexisting on a natural level. Achieving this balance does not have to come at the cost of your garden aesthetic.

What do I mean by a well-balanced garden?

Nature truly is incredible. For nearly every natural problem nature encounters, it has its own natural solution. However, nature is heavily interconnected, and for these natural solutions to be effective, there has to be minimal external interference. Interference at any stage is just like removing a brick in a game of Jenga: the whole system can come crashing down. The more bricks you remove the more likely it is the pile will collapse. That is often the issue with our gardens. Us humans tend to be a massive external interference. In the past the response to any problem our garden encountered has often been to use rather aggressive controls. Returning to my Jenga example, these aggressive controls are essentially ripping out a layer of bricks from the stack. Sure, you might win the round, but the more we interfere with the stack, the more likely it is to eventually collapse. The new and, in my opinion better, approach is less about removing or controlling, but rather to help enhance and encourage natural balances. This is the equivalent of adding more supports around your stack of Jenga bricks, meaning you can build a larger, more stable stack that can withstand more blocks being removed without collapsing.

How does a well-balanced garden work?

I will say it loud and I will say it proud: having an organic, well-balanced garden is the number one 'pest control' you can have. So how does this work?

Put simply, a balanced garden is in essence a balanced food chain. As long as there is any form of ecosystem, you will always have 'pests' in your garden. Instead of using sprays and chemicals to remove that batch of 'pests', a natural balance of predators will always be far more effective at dealing with them. Natural predators also have the added benefit of doing very little wider collateral damage too. Yes, I like hedgehogs in the garden because I have a soft spot for them, but they are also ferocious slug hunters! Sure, I love to sit and watch my wildlife pond on a warm summer's day, but under the surface it is a breeding ground for predatory insects and amphibians, both helping to keep more damaging insects under control. This can be achieved in gardens of all shapes, and even elevations. You may be thinking this is impossible to achieve in a space such a balcony on a high-rise flat, but you simply need to think about what creatures will visit your space. You might not get deer and hedgehogs, but you will most certainly still get insects, and they can be controlled by birds.

The aim of the game is to have a balanced number of creatures at each level of the food chain. If we remove all the 'pests' we indirectly remove all the predators. Then when these 'pests' return, which they will, there are no predators to keep them under control. This is where situations get out of control, and you see explosions of creatures such as aphids. Once this has happened, us gardeners are then tempted to reach for the pesticide bottle, which only accelerates the problem further.

If your garden comes under attack from creatures such as aphids, who will suck the sap out of your plants, causing them to weaken, your problem is not the aphids. Your problem is the lack of predatory insects such as ladybirds and lacewings. Instead of looking to remove all the aphids, look to invite in predatory insects. If your plants seem to get destroyed by caterpillars, again they are not the issue. Instead, your garden could do with a few more birds, especially from the tit family. A little fun fact is a single blue tit chick can eat over a hundred caterpillars per day, and each nest can contain ten or more chicks, which can mean adult blue tits need to find over a thousand caterpillars per day!

By thinking in this way, over time you will build a garden that is rich and diverse in creatures as well as plant life. You will in essence build your own little ecosystem. Not only is it brilliant to spot all the various wildlife, but you are giving wildlife a lifeline at a time when it really needs one. Funnily enough, the more wildlife you encourage into your garden, the less the wildlife in your garden becomes a problem, and that is how a well-balanced garden works.

Important note
There is one exception to this method of gardening. Over the years we have upset the natural balance by introducing certain animals into areas where they have no natural predators. These animals cannot be maintained by natural balance and they will instead upset the balance. In this situation more direct controls may need to be used. However, avoid using controls that have a lot of collateral damage.

How quickly can I achieve a balanced garden?

I would be lying if I said this was an overnight process. An easy process, yes, a fast process, no. I have been building my garden ecosystem for the last ten years. It took at least two to show any signs at all of it working, and another two before I could actually see the process working. In my garden, I would say it probably took around six years to become pretty much balanced. However, in other areas this will be considerably faster. Where I live the wildlife had been heavily damaged, and as a result I was starting off with very little. In fact, I believe most of the creatures calling my garden home today were most likely born or hatched in my garden.

It is easy to read the time it takes, and be completely put off. However, I promise you, a few years of struggle is well worth the reward at the end. My garden at home is packed full of a range of creatures, some of which are heavily endangered. This abundance of wildlife means I no longer have to worry too much about 'pest control'. I can sit back and enjoy watching nature work its magic. Yes, I lose the odd crop here and there, and I might have to use the odd net to protect certain crops. But the garden is never overrun to a level where it becomes a big problem.

I have recently taken over an allotment. The previous owner of my plot was of the opinion that anything that moved on the plot had to go. Unfortunately for me the plot has been operated in that manner for decades. As a result, I started with a barren patch of land, with practically no life whatsoever! Fast forward seven months to today, and it is well on its way to becoming a balanced plot. It was a painful few months, with a lot of damage to the crops, as inevitably the traditional adage proved right: pests will always come before the predators, as without the pests the predators have no reason to be there. However, we still managed to get a fantastic harvest, and now the plot is alive with smaller predators too. It has achieved a balance much faster than my garden, mainly due to the fact the rest of the allotment plots nearby already had an abundance of creatures ready to move in, and get the whole cycle started.

Small garden vs large garden

You may think it is easier to achieve a balanced garden in a bigger space. Yes, it is true, the larger the space available, the more you can do to bring in wildlife. More space means more habitat for creatures to call home. However, looking at it another way, the larger your garden, the more wildlife it needs to balance.

Smaller spaces are as important when it comes to providing wildlife with a home. In fact, a row of smaller gardens all working together to help give wildlife a home is just as effective as one larger garden, and possibly more so! Balconies play a vital role too. Many of the creatures we rely on are airborne. Pollinators and birds will happily use your balcony. By letting them do this you are also helping those animals who will not directly use your balcony, as they may rely on those that do.

Every country, or even different parts of the same country will have different wildlife. But the basic concept remains the same.

Build it and they will come!

Talking about why it is a good idea to encourage wildlife into your garden is important, but now let's have some fun and have a look at a few ways and DIY projects we can use to attract the wildlife in. In all honesty, this does not have to be complicated, all you need to do is make sure there is a food source, a water supply and shelter. If these three components are present in your garden, before you know it, a vast array of animals will be lining up to enter.

In the next chapter we will explore the wonderful world of rewilding (see page 187). This is where we will look at more overarching ways to help everything, by using different plants and gardening techniques to help bring all wildlife together. In this chapter I want to instead explore more targeted methods of bringing in individual groups of wildlife.

Feeder insects: what are they?

I would class feeder insects as any insect (or mollusc!) that enters the garden to feed on your plants. These include a vast array of creatures, but some of the more common ones are aphids, blackfly, slugs and caterpillars.

Why are they important?

These feeder insects are the first step on the food chain. Without them the whole garden ecosystem comes crashing down. Some of these feeder insects, such as caterpillars, are also the young of some very important pollinators.

How to attract?

Just by having a garden with plants will be enough to attract these creatures. Some plants will be better at this than others, as many gardeners know. Brassicas are vulnerable to caterpillars, aphids love a rose, slugs love hostas and blackfly are drawn to broad beans! My suggestion is to plant a mix of plants and you will soon have a mix of feeder insects.

Other invertebrates: what are they?

These are the majority of the insects we find in the garden, including many of the feeder insects spoken about previously. This includes a huge number of creatures, but a few of the most prevalent are bees, wasps, lacewings, ladybirds, butterflies, moths, hoverflies and beetles.

Why are they important?

Invertebrates in the garden have three main roles. Some invertebrates, such as lacewings, hoverflies, ladybirds and wasps, are predatory in nature. They will play a vital role in hunting insects, which will help control their populations.

Garden invertebrates also are our main plant pollinators. We all know how important bees, butterflies and moths are to pollination. But even insects such as beetles and earwigs will help to pollinate as they move from plant to plant.

While many of these creatures are predators in their own right, many are prey too. They provide a valuable food source for a range of larger animals, such as small mammals, reptiles, amphibians and birds.

How to attract?

The most effective way to bring a wide variety of invertebrates into your garden is to plant a wide and varied selection of plants and flowers. Different pollinators will like different flowers. For example, my local butterflies love buddleia, bumble bees enjoy my foxgloves and honey bees love my pear tree blossom. We will have a look at this in a bit more detail in the next chapter.

I cannot think of a more bug-rich area of my garden than my compost heap! Worms, beetles, spiders, woodlice and so many more will call this home. Not only are they helping the composting process, but they are providing rich pickings for birds and other predators.

Make an insect hotel

This is such a fun activity, and it will actually work! I have them dotted all around the garden, where they are full of solitary bees, beetles and earwigs. So how do you make one? There are so many ways to do this, but I enjoy making the one here.

Step 1: Using wood (I use old pallet wood), screw together a very simple frame with compartments, but make sure you leave the front completely open.

Step 2: Start to build out the insect rooms. To do this place various materials into the frame. As you can see, I like to use old bamboo canes, wood with holes drilled in, twigs and pine cones. But you can get creative and add in other things such as straw and old leaves.

Step 3: Hang this hotel in your garden and wait for the visitors to arrive. Solitary bees will soon fill up the holes in the bamboo canes, earwigs will enjoy the straw and beetles often enjoy everything!

Amphibians: what are they?

The most common amphibians you will see in the garden are frogs and toads. In some parts of the world, you will come across salamanders and newts too.

Why are they important?

They are prolific invertebrate hunters. A small colony of amphibians will keep insect levels under control, and they will prevent them from taking over the garden. If you are struggling with slugs, then a healthy frog population will soon get them under control. If ants are more of your problem, then a toad might be your new best friend!

Smaller amphibians are also a vital prey source for many birds, reptiles and mammals, making them an important part of the garden food cycle.

How to attract?

Ultimately, if you want amphibians in your garden, you will need an area of still water, ideally with no fish. This can be a large lake, down to a small barrel and everything in between. It is essential there is a way for them to get in and out of the water. Sloping banks are ideal, or a plank they can climb up will work too.

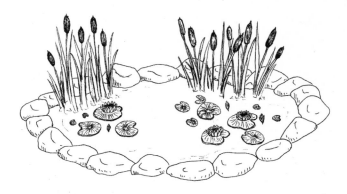

How to make a small-space amphibian pond

Step 1: Find a watertight container no smaller than 50 litres (11 gallons). This can be any container, but I like to use wooden barrels that have been cut in half.

Step 2: Dig down into the ground until the top of the container is level with the ground. This is essential, otherwise the amphibians cannot get into the pond. If you cannot dig into the ground, they will need some form of ramp, such as a log pile, to help them climb in and out.

Step 3: Fill up the container with dechlorinated water, and add in a range of plants around the container to provide shelter. Place a small ramp inside the container so they can easily exit the pond too.

Step 4: I recommend adding a water lily or bricks to the pond, so the amphibians have somewhere to rest above the surface.

Once you have a population of amphibians, they will enjoy living in your compost heaps, in log piles, and even the greenhouse. All of these locations provide the perfect damp and humid conditions they enjoy.

Every greenhouse I have ever owned has had a resident frog, enjoying the warm humid environment.

Top tip

*Frogs and toads often fall victim to the lawn mower's blade.
I like to have a quick walk around the garden before I mow, to
look for any that might be in the way. Also try to avoid mowing
after rainfall, as that is when they seem to be most active,
plus it is not a good idea to mow wet lawns as the blades will
struggle to cut the grass. It is always a good idea to leave a
section of your garden to grow wild too, where they will be safe
from the mower.*

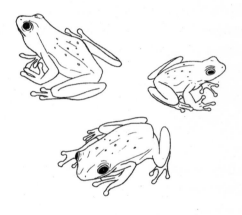

Small mammals

Other than birds and insects, small mammals are probably our most common garden friends. They are also some of our most favourite garden visitors. Different countries have a vast range of different mammals that venture into our gardens, but some common ones in my UK garden include: voles, mice, weasels, shrews, moles, squirrels, bats, hedgehogs, deer, racoon and rabbits.

Why are they important?

Mammals are both incredibly important predators and prey. Many, such as hedgehogs, will help keep insect populations under control, while others, such as mice, are vital prey for larger predators.

How to attract?

Due to their vast array of natural predators, small mammals are naturally wary animals. It is crucial to offer them as much cover as possible. Fallen leaves, twigs and log piles are all fantastic hiding spots for small mammals. They will also appreciate hedge-rows and overgrown areas.

Many mammals will also appreciate a safe place to nest. I have various bird boxes around the garden and every year the one in my hedge-row will be inhabited by mice.

Build your own hedgehog/ small mammal house

This can be as simple as a large pile of twigs, for them to burrow into, or even better, a purpose-built wooden house. Building a hedgehog house can be as easy or complex as you would like to make it. If you fancy a bit of a challenge, consider building a wooden hedgehog box, or alternatively you can attempt to make one from twigs and leaves.

Wooden hedgehog house

Step 1: Gather some wooden planks together that are no longer than 60 cm (2 feet) long; old pallet wood is ideal for this.

Step 2: Nail or screw together your planks to create a box at least 30 cm (1 foot) square in size.

Step 3: Place another plank over the top (or place two connected planks like in the drawing) to create a simple roof.

Step 4: Cut out an entrance hole big enough for the hedgehogs or other mammals to fit through.

Step 5: Screw four more smaller wooden planks together, to create a tunnel for the entrance.

Step 6: Fill this box with a mix of fallen autumn leaves, hay and straw, this will act as a natural bedding.

Step 7: Place this house in a sheltered spot in your garden, and wait for the new inhabitants to move in. You may even get some hibernating over the winter months!

Step 8: Once a year (at a time where nothing is living inside), clean out the box with a gentle soapy solution, to avoid the chance of any disease build up.

It is also a good idea to speak to your neighbours about building a hedgehog/small mammal highway. This is as simple as cutting a small hole in the bottom of the garden fences. That way mammals can travel freely between gardens.

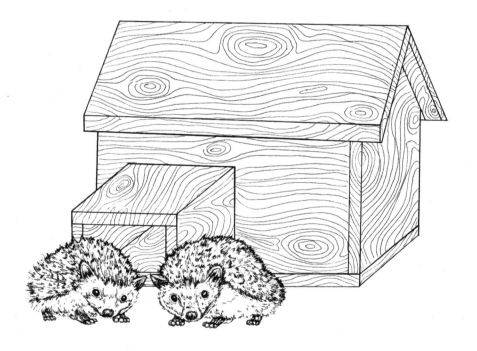

Fallen twigs and leaves hedgehog house

Step 1: Gather up a large bundle of fallen twigs.

Step 2: Choose a nice quiet corner of the garden that you will not need to disturb throughout the winter.

Step 3: Start to pile up your twigs, I like to make my pile at least 30 cm (12 in) high.

Step 4: Another option I like is to gather some fallen autumn leaves and sprinkle these all over and around the twigs. Hedgehogs and other creatures will use this pile to make their own nests, therefore there is no need to make it neat, as they will rearrange it themselves.

Top tip

Bonfire piles make the ideal home for lots of garden creatures, especially small mammals. We also tend to have bonfires right around the time many are looking for a safe place to hibernate. Please, always check your bonfire piles before lighting them, as chances are there will be a few animals calling it home, especially if it has been there for a few weeks. I would recommend getting a metal burn bin instead.

Garden birds

I would place a bet, at least in the UK, that other than insects, birds will be the most common visitor to your garden. It is quite funny; the older I get the more I understand and appreciate the joys of bird watching! I have noted all the birds I have seen in my garden and the list is more than sixty species long. Some of the most common birds found in our gardens are pigeons, blue tits (as well as many other members of the tit family), song thrushes, woodpeckers, hawks, robins, starlings, crows, kingfishers and humming birds. Where you are in the world will change what species you will see.

Why are they important?

Birds play a vital role in our garden ecosystem. They are efficient hunters, helping to control a vast number of insects. Unlike most mammals, except for perhaps bats, birds have the ability to catch airborne bugs as well as ground
bugs. The tit family are incredible at removing caterpillars from your plants, and if snails and slugs are your issue, then invite a song thrush into your garden.

Some birds are also prey, usually to other birds such as hawks, but often larger predators such as foxes. This helps to maintain a healthy balance in the garden. If birds were left unchecked, they would soon make short work of the insects in our gardens.

While not found in the UK, for my American friends, hummingbirds play a vital role in the pollination of plants.

The world would be a very boring place without birdsong. Not too long ago, I went to a province in France where small birds had been hunted to near extinction. It was eerie. My whole life has been lived with a theatrical chorus of birdsong. It was strange how much I missed the little critters and their background noise. Since then, I have not taken a single one for granted.

How to attract?

Like mammals, birds need shelter, food and water. The best way to bring birds into your garden is by planting trees, as this offers all three. We discuss this in more detail in chapter 8 (see page 212).

Birds need to feel safe before they will come in to feed. If you have a bird feeder in the middle of your garden, it will not be visited as regularly as if it was placed in a more sheltered area. Watching birds come in to feed on my bird tables is fascinating. They will land in a nearby tree or hedge, then wait for a few minutes while they check the coast is clear before coming in to feed.

I recommend putting a bird feeding station in a secluded corner of the garden. When feeding birds, it is important to have a mix of hanging bird feeders, as well as flat trays with food. Some birds cannot feed off the hanging feeders so they rely on the flat trays and tables. Make sure to feed a mix of seeds to suit the different beak sizes. During the spring and early summer when the birds have young it is a good idea to provide the birds with food that has a high moisture content, such as live mealworms. Young birds rely on the moisture from the food to survive. Just a word of caution when using bird feeders, and that is they will often become over run with squirrels. This is something I personally do not mind, but if you want to avoid this issue make sure to purchase a squirrel-resistant bird feeder. These come in many different forms, but most commonly have either a cage around the feeder that only small birds can get through, or a counterweight perch that only opens to reveal the food inside when a bird is sat on it, weighing it down.

Important note

A dirty bird feeder is far worse than no bird feeder at all! Dirty bird feeders often spread salmonella and other viruses and disease. Make sure to clean your bird feeders regularly, with warm natural soapy water.

While I have lots of bird boxes around the garden, many of which are used every year to house a new bird family, I prefer to offer natural ways for them to build their own nests. As I cannot speak bird I will never truly know, but I get the impression they prefer to build their own too. So how can you help?

Gather some natural materials such as wool, hair, twigs, moss and straw/hay. Either place in a wire bird feeder or bundle it together with natural twine. With both versions, just make sure birds can easily pull out what they need. Hang your bundles out in the garden and before you know it (especially in early spring) they will be stripped bare. You will see countless birds flying around with all sorts of materials in their beaks as they get to work building their nests.

A word of caution

While I recommend we invite nature into our gardens we do need to operate a little caution. Please remember I live in the UK, where we have very few animals that can hurt you. Apart from one species of venomous snake, a wasp is about as bad as it gets. I recommend you use a slight degree of common sense. If you live in an area where mosquitos carry disease, then building a wildlife pond may not be the best idea. Also, while predators are a sign of a healthy garden, again, where I live the biggest and most fearsome is a badger, yes, a badger. I am not dealing with very large predators that can pose a risk to your safety. As mentioned earlier, everything is welcome in my garden; the good, the annoying and the slimy. But if you live somewhere a bit richer in nature than the UK, then I understand that this approach might not be quite as sensible.

Organic controls

I understand the pain of certain creatures working their way through your crops. In the process of building a balanced garden I lost hundreds of plants, and even now, with a balanced garden, I will still lose a few each year. Sometimes even the most balanced gardens will have factors outside of its control, which can cause an influx of damaging creatures. A great example was a recent spring in my own garden. This spring was an unusually wet and humid one. Both of these conditions are perfect for slugs and snails to thrive. Oh, and boy did they thrive! The slugs especially came with a vengeance, causing some damage to my early sowings. The problem was, it was too early. The hedgehogs were not fully active, neither were the frogs and toads. That just left the birds, and they struggled to control these slugs without the back up of small mammals and amphibians.

This is a rare occurrence, but when it does happen, you feel the need to intervene. In these situations it is not necessarily a bad thing, as you are simply restoring the balance, but please, whatever you do, try to avoid the temptation of chemical control. Using pesticides to fix individual issues is like trying to catch a fish using dynamite. Sure, chances are you might catch the fish you wanted, but you will also kill everything else nearby. Instead, here are a few organic controls you can try:

NETS

Nets are a gardener's best friend. They come in all shapes and sizes, and all different materials. If you are really struggling to keep insects away from certain crops, try using a very fine-mesh net. Nets are also great to keep rabbits away from leafy greens and birds away from soft fruit. But remember to provide these animals with food elsewhere.

BEER TRAPS

If slugs are really causing you to tear your hair out, then try to use a few beer traps. Bury a small container such as an old opened tin, so the top is level with the soil. Pop a little bit of beer in the bottom of the container, and wait overnight. The slugs will be drawn in by the beer, where they will then fall in and cannot escape.

SHARP BARRIERS

You can help to slow the damage from slugs and snails by placing sharp barriers around your plants. I like to use very spiky brambles with very sharp spikes, but I have seen people use crushed eggshells and sharp gravel.

SACRIFICIAL PLANTING

There are just some plants certain creatures cannot resist. A great example of two of these plants are nasturtiums and marigolds. No matter what I plant the slugs seem to find the marigolds first, and will always attack them. Nasturtiums seem to be a favourite place for the brassica butterfly to lay their eggs. You can plant these and other sacrificial plants next to your crops, and this can help to keep these little critters off the prized plants.

REMOVE BY HAND

Often the best way to deal with an influx of certain creatures is to simply remove them by hand. Pop on a pair of gardening gloves and inspect your plants. You can crush aphids and blackflies between your fingers. If slugs are the problem, head out with a torch at night, and trust me you will catch them in the act.

COPPER TOOLS/TAPE

Some gardeners swear by copper's ability to repel slugs and snails. While this method has never fully been backed up by science, it may be worth a try.

BLAST WITH WATER

For smaller infestations, on more sturdy plants, you can simply use the jet setting on your hose pipe attachment to blast any creatures off. This is especially effective against aphids.

GARLIC AND SOAP SPRAY

You can make your own weak garlic and soap plant spray to help keep unwanted insects off crops such as cabbages. The aroma of the garlic helps to deter insects, and the soap allows it to stick to the leaves. Simply crush a few garlic cloves and place in about half a litre (a pint) of water. Leave this overnight and then strain into a spray bottle. Add in a tiny drop of washing-up liquid and you are ready to go!

SHINY OBJECTS

You can attach shiny objects such as old CDs and tin-foil pots to string and hang in the garden. These will blow in the wind, helping to scare off birds. I prefer not to do this and would instead net any crops you want to protect from birds.

Just remember, it is best to only use these methods to bring a certain creature back into balance. Then let nature do its thing again. If you start going too far, you will undo all the hard work you have done by trying to balance your garden. As a balanced garden will always be by far the best method of control possible.

Bee kind to bees!

I do not like to put garden creatures into a hierarchy, but I have to put bees as top priority when it comes to giving wildlife a helping hand. Bees are essential to our survival as a species. Put simply, no bees, no us! Over one-third of the food we eat is pollinated by bees, and three-quarters of our food relies on bees in some way. It is estimated in the UK alone bees contribute over £1 billion to the economy.

Despite their importance, bees are facing so many threats at the moment. The industrial use of pesticides, combined with habitat loss and a rapidly changing climate, has caused a dramatic decrease in their numbers. Pesticides can be especially damaging to bees. While most bees are actually solitary, some work as a hive. When bees are out pollinating crops that have been sprayed with pesticides, they will then take it back to the hive. This causes the whole colony to become affected, and it is often completely wiped out as a result. Closer to home, bees also do the majority of the pollinating in our gardens. Some plants, such as tomatoes, are almost entirely dependent on bees as pollinators.

So, what can us gardeners do to help out? I think changing people's attitude towards bees is the best first step. Still to this day I see people swat at bees and try to run from them, in fear of getting stung. Unlike a wasp, a bee is not really interested in you, as they have better things to do. I am around bees all day every day for my job, and I have only ever been stung once, which I may add was completely my own fault! I decided to walk across my clover lawn barefooted, and inevitably I stood on one, poor little thing! I want to say this as many times as I can; a bee will never sting you for no reason, only if it is very threatened, as in my case when my giant flipper was coming down on top of it. Once people are on board that bees are friends and not foe, we can look at a few more ways to help out, including:

GROWING SOME FOOD AT HOME

Food that has been grown organically at home will help to reduce the amount of sprayed food we need to buy from the shops.

PLANT A MIXTURE OF FLOWERS

This is a topic we will explore in detail in the next chapter (see page 199). Different bees will have different abilities, and therefore can pollinate different flowers. Bumblebees, for example, have longer tongues than honey bees. By planting a mix of flowers, you will accommodate a range of bees, and offer them different food sources, at different times of the year. Aim for longer displays, over massive vibrant, but fleeting, displays.

GIVE SOLITARY BEES A HOME

The insect hotel we built earlier in this chapter (see page 164) is perfect for this. You can even go simpler and just drill a few holes into a log.

AVOID MOWING YOUR LAWN

When we mow our lawns, we also cut down quite a few flowers, such as daisies and clovers. Both of these are a fantastic food source for our local bees.

PROVIDE BEES WITH A SAFE SPACE TO DRINK

Like all living creatures, bees need to drink water. The best way to offer bees a drink is to use a bird bath, or saucer, and place rocks into the water. Make sure these rocks break through the surface of the water. These rocks will provide the bees a safe place to land, and drink, without fear of drowning. Just make sure to swap out the water every few days to keep it fresh.

AVOID USING PESTICIDES IN THE GARDEN

At this point in the chapter, this probably goes without saying! It is never a good idea to use pesticides in the garden. While you are probably not aiming to harm any bees, they will most definitely become collateral damage.

Top tip

If you see a bee looking a bit sorry for itself on the ground, then chances are it has run out of energy. This is common in early spring, when their natural food sources are often quite scarce. To help them, mix 2 teaspoons of white granulated sugar with 1 teaspoon of water, and leave out next to the bee. You will see their tongue start to lap up the mixture, and soon they will be on their way again. Never give them honey!

Good news story

Buzz Stops! New bee bus stops arriving on a street near you.

The Wildlife Trusts and Clear Channel in the UK have partnered up to give nature a helping hand in our urban areas.

Clear Channel, a leading media infrastructure company, signed a five-year deal with The Wildlife Trusts to help bring our cities' bus stops to life.

Their plan is to add a natural green roof, full of plants and flowers, to these bus stops. This project will run up and down the full length of the UK. The roofs will help transform our urban areas into a more friendly place for urban pollinators, which will hopefully give their numbers a boost.

These wild roofs have been assessed for their impact on wildlife and deemed to be of 'high strategic significance'. The Wildlife Trusts will be providing expert knowledge to make sure the greenbus stop roofs are placed in the areas that need it the most.

Hopefully, the success of these living roofs will encourage more countries and communities to follow suit and add a bit more greenery to our grey urban areas.

Checklist

Have your notebook and pencil handy to make a note of your answers to the following prompts:

→ What wildlife have you seen in your garden?

→ What other wildlife do you wish to attract?

→ List what you have done to help encourage local wildlife into your garden.

→ What would you like to build next?

→ What animals or insects have caused the most damage in your garden?

→ Do these animals have a natural predator you can encourage? If so, list them.

→ Have you noticed a decrease in pests?

7

Go wild and rewild

Rewilding is a hot topic right now. Head to any flower show, and many show gardens on display will have an element of rewilding incorporated into them. It is a method of gardening I have been deploying in my garden for years, long before I even knew what it was called.

So just what is rewilding? Put simply, it is returning a patch of land to a more natural state. Due to human interference, most gardens are not very natural at all. I mean, in how many parts of the natural world will you find perfectly manicured grass, with carefully carved out flower borders where each flower is growing perfectly spaced apart? The natural world tends to be a bit more chaotic. This makes gardens the perfect projects to incorporate a little element of rewilding.

In the previous chapter we looked at a few direct ways to help bring in certain wildlife, such as feeding birds with bird feeders and making man-made shelters. Rewilding, on the other hand, is far more overarching in its ability to help nature. I believe it could be the single most powerful way we can use our gardens as a force for good.

If I am being honest, I never really understood the traditional approach to gardening. I have always seen more beauty in a little bit of natural mess, packed full of life, than in perfectly manicured gardens, devoid of any animals other than perhaps the family pet. I would just like to clarify, by natural mess I do not mean being lazy and abandoning your garden. Instead, I mean trying not to get too trigger happy with the pruning, mowing and weeding.

As a child I distinctly remember being really bad at weeding. My great-grandmother and I would set out to weed a flower border together, only for our respective sections to look completely different.

My nan's section would be very traditional, nice and neat, with not a weed in sight. Whereas mine, well, pretty much everything stayed as it was. You see, in my garden, many of these so-called weeds are plants such as dandelions, clovers and buttercups, all of which have beautiful flowers. These flowers were stunning and packed full of bees. I could not, and still cannot, see the logic in removing these 'weeds' that were in bloom just to make room for flowers you hope will bloom later on. Back then, as I was always reminded, this was called bad gardening. Now it is called rewilding, and this approach is winning gold medals at the world's most prestigious flower shows! Sometimes it is funny how things work out.

How to rewild your garden

In the previous chapter we explained why it is so important to give wildlife a helping hand, and the importance of a balanced garden; so now let's jump straight in and have a look at a few ways we can make our gardens wilder.

I should quickly mention that while rewilding will obviously help local wildlife, it can also help to control temperatures, fight climate change and reduce flooding too.

All of the projects in the previous chapter (such as building bird feeders) count as rewilding, but here are a few more overarching, garden-wide ways we can rewild.

Use natural instead of man-made

Our gardens are often full of man-made structures such as concrete walkways, wooden fences and tiled patios. Instead, try to think of a more natural way to achieve the same result. I would suggest swapping concrete paths for woodchip, using shingle for your patio and, my favourite, swap fences for hedges.

These more natural solutions come with so many benefits to your garden, including:

* Fewer hard surfaces. Hard surfaces do not allow rainfall to permeate through to the soil below. Instead, any heavy rainfall will start to puddle, and this will often lead to a large amount of surface runoff. If your garden has too much surface runoff, and this water has nowhere to go, then before you know it, you will have some flooding to deal with.

* Living barriers such as trees and hedges will help to replace carbon dioxide with oxygen. This is a topic we will explore in far more detail in the next chapter.

* Natural alternatives will provide precious shelter for wildlife. Hedges and shrubs are home to all sorts of birds and small mammals, and woodchip paths will be the perfect hiding spot for myriad small invertebrates.

* Hedges have the added benefit of letting smaller animals pass through them, unlike solid fences.

* Some bushes, such as hawthorns, will produce flowers, which will provide another food source for your local pollinators.

Top tip

If you are planting a hedgerow along a boundary line, make sure to plant it a little way inside of the line. It will soon bush out to fill the gap without spilling into your neighbour's property.

Keep your lawn mower in the shed

We seem to have a bit of an obsession with well-manicured lawns. Grass in our lawns is possibly the most common form of plants in our gardens, but trimming them to within an inch of their life every week is not great for our local wildlife. When we mow our lawns, we are not just chopping grass, quite a few small flowers, such as clovers, dandelions, daisies and buttercups, are often growing among the grass too. When we mow the lawn, we mow these flowers as well. However, these small flowers are often an early lifeline for many pollinators. Take dandelions, for example, they are one of the first flowers to appear in my garden in early spring, providing a lifeline for any early bees. The mower in a few minutes can remove all of this valuable food for our pollinators.

Many small creatures rely on tall grass for shelter in the garden. Long grass will almost create a natural highway for them to use, without the fear of being attacked by predators. Not only will the long grass help bring in more life to the garden, but it will help that wildlife move around the garden too.

Keeping the mowers tucked away in the shed during times of high animal activity and plant growth seasons, such as spring and summer, will help to save quite a few unfortunate accidental deaths.

> **Important note**
> *The larger the area of lawn you leave to grow wild, the better. However, even by leaving a small strip or corner to grow wild, you will still be helping out.*

Leave some weeds

The word weed is similar to the word pest in the previous chapter. I don't believe it is a beneficial word to use in the garden. It automatically labels certain plants as problematic, and suggests they therefore need to be removed. The ironic part is, many of these so-called weeds provide vital food for our pollinators.

What I find slightly strange is that many of the weeds we remove from our flower borders actually have better blooms than our carefully planted bedding plants. Thistles, daisies, buttercups, clovers and dandelions all produce stunning flowers. I often think that if we sowed a packet of thistle seeds we would be over the moon with their floral display, but the minute they pop up uninvited, many gardeners deem them to be weeds and rip them out.

Some weeds are useful for a range of other reasons. Nettles are common in gardens across the globe. For whatever reason we have deemed they are weeds and they are often removed. Not only are nettles a fantastic home for a range of wildlife, but as we saw in chapter five of this book, they make fantastic plant food (see page 134).

However, this does not mean you need to let your entire garden become overrun with weeds. Some areas of the garden and weeds are not a good combination, such as your vegetable patch. When removing any weeds please avoid using any weed killers. Instead, try using:

* A weed-suppressing membrane. Laid on the soil around the plants this will block out light, which helps keep many weeds at bay.

* Mulching. This is the process of adding organic matter such as compost or leaf mould to your beds and borders. Mulch can help to suppress quite a few smaller weeds.

* The good old-fashioned garden hoe. Garden hoes come in all shapes and sizes and are one of the most useful garden tools you can have. A quick skim along the soil surface with a hoe will pop out the majority of weeds.

Important note
Not all weeds can be treated in the same way. While dandelions and nettles are pretty harmless, and are actually quite useful, others can pose quite a dangerous risk. Weeds such as giant hogweed and Japanese knotweed are far more of a problem. For these more problematic plants, I recommend enlisting the help of a specialist, and in the case of knotweed it is actually a legal requirement in the UK to do so, due to the structural damage it can cause to buildings.

Avoid being too tidy

Other than using pesticides, having a tidy garden is possibly the worst thing you can do for your local wildlife. Neat borders, perfectly pruned plants and manicured lawns may seem like the ideal garden, but dig a little deeper and a lot of garden wildlife will be missing. By being overly neat in your garden you risk removing all the natural highways, shelters, homes and food for the wildlife trying to thrive in your small patch of earth. Now this does not mean you should let your garden become a total mess, but rather consider leaving a little bit of natural mess. This could include:

* Leaving some dead flower heads, as they will offer seeds for the birds to eat.

* When clearing up fallen autumn leaves, consider leaving a few small piles dotted around the garden, as small animals will use this as shelter.

* Maybe leave the pruning alone for a little bit. As long as trees and shrubs are not causing any danger, or intruding into neighbours' property, then let some of them grow wild.

* As long as it is not causing any danger, consider leaving anything that has blown down in the wind. This can range from leaves and fruit, to entire branches. The local wildlife will always find a way to utilize it.

Time to get wild about wildflowers

Possibly the best way to rewild your garden is by creating a wildflower meadow. Sure, traditional flower borders packed full of your typical garden flowers are great, but in regards to helping your local wildlife, they do not even come close to wildflowers.

Many of the popular flowers we see in gardens around the globe are simply modified versions of wildflowers. A great example of this can be seen with roses. We often associate roses with large blooms of intricate petals, often with a heavy scent. These roses, which are usually hybrid tea roses, are a man-made creation. If you see a more traditional rose (often called species roses), such as a dog rose, you will notice a massive difference. Species roses will usually have a far simpler petal formation, which is much more inviting to your local pollinators.

This pattern of human interference with flowers is pretty common, and unfortunately it often has a negative impact on wildlife. Ultimately,

Hybrid tea rose

Wildflower rose

we have been breeding flowers to sell, and to make flowers more attractive to consumers, flower heads are becoming increasingly intricate, with complex petal formations. You might see this phrased as double petal flowers. I have to admit, many of these double petal flowers look stunning. However, these flowers are not ideal for the majority of pollinators, as they struggle to reach the nectar inside.

Now I would be a hypocrite if I said I did not love these modern flowers! I do, and I always will, as they are just fantastic to look at. Rewilding your flower border does not mean you need to rip out your favourite varieties of hybrid flowers. Instead, we should consider mixing in a few older native species, or even making a wildflower meadow as well.

In the last one hundred years, the UK has lost nearly ninety-seven per cent of our native wildflower meadows, and in other countries it is a similar picture. Wildflower meadows act as an all-you-can-eat buffet for pollinators, as well as a rich habitat for all sorts of other creatures too. It is pretty obvious to see where this is going: no wildflower meadows, fewer pollinators; the fewer the pollinators, the harder it is to grow and produce our food.

Luckily, smaller wildflower meadows planted in our gardens and even window boxes can help. While very few gardens are large enough to create a giant wildflower meadow, together as a collective group us gardeners can make all the difference. It is easy to think your small wildflower meadow is not making a difference, but remember, there are millions of gardens in every country, and if each one added a small wildflower meadow, you will soon create a fragmented but massive meadow, packed full of wildlife.

CREATING YOUR MINI WILDFLOWER MEADOW

There is a common misconception that you need acres of land to create a wildflower meadow. Yes, it is true, the larger the space the more impactful your wildflower meadow will be, but this does not mean we should give up if we do not have a massive garden. In fact, quite the opposite! Every garden from a window box to rolling acres and everything in between will help bring our wildflower meadows back from the brink.

WHERE TO START?

You will need a place to grow your wildflower meadow. I would recommend open ground, but if you live in a flat or have a very small garden you can get creative; I have sowed wildflowers in all sorts of containers in the past. Here are a few ideas on where to start your wildflower meadow:

* Garden borders
* Unused corner in your garden
* Raised beds
* Large containers
* Window boxes
* Use old sinks and bathtubs
* Ask your local council if you can plant on any verges outside your home

GROWING CONDITIONS

The majority of wildflower seed mixes will contain plants what will grow best in full sun. Make sure the area you have selected for your wildflowers is open and sunny. If you have a shaded garden, but still want to grow a selection of wildflowers, try to find a woodland mix. This will contain a range of plants that are far more suited to shaded conditions.

Unlike the vast majority of other plants in your garden, many wildflowers will grow best in poorer soil, where they are not competing with other plants. Try to avoid growing in areas of the garden that are rich in organic matter or have recently had fertilizer added.

If your soil is rich, try to remove the top 15 cm (6 in) of topsoil. I would avoid placing this topsoil in your vegetable containers or raised beds, as it will most likely contain quite a few weed seeds. Instead, you can scatter it in areas of the garden where you are not trying to grow flowers or crops. I often sprinkle it over my lawn, rake it so it is even and then throw some fresh grass seed over the top, which will give your lawn a little boost.

LET'S SOW

There are a range of different wildflower seed options you can buy, and if you have a little bit of experience, you can even make your own. However, I highly recommend buying a wildflower seed mix from your local area, as these will contain a higher level of native plants. You can even buy small plug plants in the spring and plant them out to create a wildflower meadow. There is no right or wrong way to start, but I recommend buying a pre-made wildflower mix from your local plant nursery.

When sowing a wildflower meadow, you can either sow your seeds in autumn or early spring. I usually sow mine in autumn for two reasons. One, there is less garden work to do, so it gives me a good excuse to head outside. Two, your wildflower will start to bloom the following spring, whereas with spring sowings you can expect to see your first-year seeds bloom later in the summer.

For the vast majority of wildflower seed mixes I like to work on a ratio of 5–8 grams of seed per square metre of space you want to fill (about a quarter of an ounce per 10 square feet).

Now we are ready to have some fun and sow our new wildflower meadow. Sowing the seeds could not be easier. Simply scatter your seed mix over the soil you have prepared earlier. Try your best to sprinkle the seeds as evenly as possible. Areas where the seed is too dense may struggle to grow, and areas with no seed can leave visible

patches in your meadow. Please do not worry too much if your seed distribution is not perfect. Over the next few years your meadow will start to self-seed, and it will settle down into a natural spacing.

Rake these seeds into the soil, then trample them in using your feet, or using your hands if you are sowing in containers. The aim of the game here is to make sure every seed has good contact with the soil.

In the vast majority of climates, the natural rainfall should provide all the water your wildflowers need. Remember, you are growing primarily native plants which are perfectly suited to your local areas weather conditions. This is the beauty of using native plants, and also a good reason why it is so important. My wildflower seed mix on the outskirts of London will look completely different to a wildflower mix for, say, Florida, or California. However, if you are experiencing unusually dry weather for your climate, it is a good idea to give them a little helping hand with a good watering.

The local birds will start to eye up your wildflower seed the minute you scatter it, especially if you sow your seeds in autumn, when their food supplies are limited. After spending the last two chapters talking about helping the birds this may seem hypocritical, but try your best to prevent this. I use nets, and if the problem is particularly bad, hang tin-foil trays, which usually do a pretty good job at sending them to the bird feeders instead. Your local birds will benefit far more from an established wildflower meadow, and all the extra creatures this will help attract, as well as all the extra seed heads that will grow. For each seed a bird eats now, it could have hundreds more in a few months' time.

MAINTAINING YOUR MEADOW

Your wildflower meadow will be without a shadow of a doubt the easiest flower border you have ever maintained. There is no weeding, or careful planting, and unlike many traditional borders that are packed full of annuals, you only need to plant it once, and it will return year on year.

In the first year of growth, chop down, or mow your meadow in mid to late summer. I like to make a bit of noise first, to give any little creatures a chance to evacuate to another area. Make sure to leave these chopped flowers on the ground for a few days, so they have a chance to drop their seeds.

After the first year, there is practically zero maintenance, other than maybe the odd water in long dry spells, and the occasional tidy up around the edges, to prevent it from taking over your garden. Each year it will need another chop just as autumn is about to set in.

Plants for bees and butterflies

Sometimes you might want to plant certain flowers to attract certain pollinators, usually bees and butterflies. While these pollinators will happily visit a wide range of plants and flowers, it is always best to look for plants that are native to your area. To see which plants these might be, contact your local wildlife trust, or conservation team, and they will be more than happy to help you.

When planting for pollinators, it is important use a mix of plants, planted at different times of the year. You could hand select the top five best flowers for bees, but if they all burst into life at the same time and die off at the same time, this is not very beneficial. Instead, try to spread out your planting, so your local pollinators have at least one option throughout the year. This is especially important at the moment due to more regular weather extremes. The late winter months where I live have been very mild recently, and I have been spotting more and more pollinators looking for food earlier and earlier each year.

Top tip

Research has shown that bees may be able to see the colour purple more clearly than other colours. Bear this in mind when selecting your flower seeds, as many of the flowers in the lists opposite will come in a range of different colours.

While your local experts can advise what is best for your area, here are a few suggestions of my favourites that I like to use. Please remember, many of these plants will come in a range of varieties. When planting with pollinators in mind, you need to avoid any double bloom/petal varieties. Yes, they may look nice, but the pollinators will often just leave them alone.

Top tip

If you want to attract butterflies, a buddleia is going to be the best option for you. They are stunning plants, with the most amazing fragrance, which the butterflies love as much as I do. They are so good at bringing butterflies into the garden that buddleias are sometimes referred to as the butterfly bush. During the summer months when mine are in bloom, I can guarantee you at any point in the day there will be at least one butterfly on it! Please keep your buddleia well pruned, as they are vigorous growers, and can even damage structures if left to their own devices.

Plants for bees	Plants for butterflies
Alliums (ES)	Aster (LS)
Apple blossom (S)	Buddleia (ES)
Aster (LS)	Cornflower (ES)
Borage (LS)	Dill (ES)
Cherry blossom (S)	Fennel (LS)
Cornflower (ES)	Goldenrod (LS)
Cosmos (LS)	Hollyhock (ES)
Crocus (S)	Honeysuckle (LS)
Dahlia (LS)	Lavender (ES)
Foxgloves (ES)	Liastris (ES)
Globe artichoke (LS)	Mallow (LS)
Hollyhock (ES)	Marigolds (ES)
Ivy (LS)	Phlox (LS)
Lavender (ES)	Privet (ES)
Marigolds (ES)	Sage (ES)
Pear blossom (S)	Snapdragon (S)
Rosemary (S)	Sunflower (ES)
Runner beans (LS)	Verbena (ES)
Sunflowers (ES)	Yarrow (LS)
Winter clematis (W)	Zinnia (LS)

Key (S) Spring flowering, (ES) Early summer flowering, (LS) Late summer flowering, (W) Winter flowering

The death of our front gardens

Hanging up in my grandad's office is an aerial picture taken above the row of houses we live in. I believe this picture was taken in the 1970s or 80s, before I was born.

In every front garden were rows and rows of flower borders, trees and hedges. One garden had a vegetable patch and another even had a pond! They were all bursting with colour, and there was not a fence panel to be seen. Instead, bushes and very small picket fences separated each plot.

Recently, in an old photo album I saw an even older picture of my street from the 1950s. What I found interesting is there seemed to be more plants in the front garden than in the back. Now looking out the window the same row of front gardens presents a pretty bleak picture. Other than mine, and my nan and grandad's front garden next door, the only colour you can see is grey. Modern life and the rise of car ownership has basically reduced many front gardens to no more than a car park.

It might be worth just adding that some of the techniques used to achieve these amazing front gardens back in the 1950smight not have been the most eco-conscious, but there is nothing to say we cannot achieve similar results today using the slightly more environmentally friendly techniques we have discussed in this book.

Putting the environmental benefits to one side for a moment, the street looked incredible in these old pictures, it was far more inviting and uplifting. On a human level, this has to impact our mental health. I don't know about you, but when I drive through an attractive little hamlet or village, filled with cottages and their pretty gardens, my mood immediately gets a boost. If, on the other hand, I am in a run-down, industrial part of town, with nothing but grey man-made structures, my mood nose dives! Is it time we stop this trend of destroying our front gardens, to turn them into car parks? I would have to say yes, it is something we should all consider, if not for the environment's sake, then at least our own. I think the world needs a little bit more joy and colour right now, and the front garden is the perfect place to start.

So why exactly have I shared this story about front gardens in a chapter about rewilding? Well, in all honesty, I think our front gardens are a prime area to start rewilding. Nature will not mind if we make them a home in the front or back garden, they will be grateful either way. So, my thinking is, instead of us all building beautiful wildflower meadows in the back garden, where only you can enjoy them, let's showcase what we are doing to the world in the front garden.

Obviously, you might need a space to park your vehicle, and for the majority of front gardens this leaves little room for anything else. But you see that is the best part about rewilding. You do not have to use the whole garden; little bits added here and there are as effective, it could even be as small as a window box on the front of your house or flat.

Motivated by what I saw in those old images, I decided to put my money were my mouth is and rewild my front garden. This was four years ago, and I think it was possibly the best advert for a more wildlife friendly approach to gardening I ever could have wished for. All I did was make four pretty small changes:

* I replaced all the fence panels with either hedgerows or picket fences.

* I planted trailing plants to grow up the walls of my house, including native roses, clematis and ivy.

* My front garden is rectangular, with one of the smaller lengths leading onto the road, and the other against the front of the house. Along both longer lengths and the short length in front of the house, I put in flower borders. In one border I planted a wildflower 'meadow', another is a bed of all different sunflowers and the third one is a bit of a mix up of different perennials, such as roses, lupins and foxgloves.

* This last one was a bit more effort, but completely worth it. I dug out the old concrete driveway, right down to the soil below, then placed a weed barrier down and laid down lots of small pebbles and shingle. Not only does this look far more natural, it also lets any heavy rainwater permeate through to the soil below. Since doing this the front garden has not flooded once.

All of this is pretty basic rewilding, and in all honesty, other than the shingle, it was pretty cheap to achieve. I was pleased with the job I had done, but I had no idea what was coming next.

Nearly everyone I knew from the local area started to comment on the front garden, and it got people talking. The wildflower borders were a firm favourite, as were the sunflowers. My bedroom window looks out over the front garden, and during the summer months I often catch passers by having a good look at the flowers. Sometimes they even take a photo, which I do not mind, in fact, I take it as a compliment. I would love to say this is due to my awesome landscaping skills, but in reality it is because the surrounding front gardens are so grey and monotone it really makes mine stand out. I will never know if I have motivated any of these people to replicate any rewilding in their gardens, but what I do know is it has raised a few people's mood as they have passed by, and brought an abundance of wildlife back into my front garden.

> **Top tip:** *Sometimes people can be put off planting or putting effort into their front gardens because the whole world can see if you have any fails. Trust me, we all fail from time to time in our gardens. Also, I promise you, nobody is monitoring your garden design that closely, only you. The bar is so low when it comes to many front gardens these days, that even the slightest bit of added colour will look amazing!*

Checklist

Have your notebook and pencil handy to make a note of your answers to the following prompts:

→ Think about what areas of the garden you would like to rewild.

→ If you have left the mower alone, have you seen an increase in wildlife?

→ What flowers in your garden do your pollinators seem to enjoy the most?

→ Make a list of any native wildflowers you like.

→ Are there any non-permeable surfaces you can change in your garden?

→ If you have a front garden, list any ways you may be able to add a bit of colour and life to it.

→ Think vertical: are there any walls or fences in your garden that you may be able to use to grow climbing plants up?

8

Trees, a garden's best friend!

Grab a shovel and your welly boots, because we are planting a tree.

At the bottom of my garden stands a pine tree. It is rather spindly, branches are missing, it never produces pine cones, and in all honesty it looks pretty hopeless! However, this is the beauty of trees. Even the ones that look pretty lifeless to us will look like a palace to nature. As I am writing this chapter, from my window I can see four different species of bird using the pine tree as a temporary resting space, checking that the coast is clear, before descending down to our bird feeders for their breakfast.

I have always had a bit of a soft spot for trees. This could be due to one of my earliest memories of being out in the summer sun with my great-grandmother, counting all the ladybirds on a Christmas tree we planted out many years prior. What is ironic is she hated the idea of trees in the garden and was always worried the big pine tree we have just mentioned was going to blow over and, in her words, 'split the house in half'. Despite it being well over 60 metres (200 feet) away from the house and only about 18 metres (60 feet) tall.

While trees can be grand and imposing, the strange thing I have noticed is no matter how large they are, they have a fantastic ability to blend in! Don't believe me? Have a little walk around your local area and pay specific attention to just the trees. No matter how long you have lived there, or how many times you have passed by, you will notice numerous large trees you have never seen before. The same will apply to your garden and local outside spaces. You may be fearful of your outside space being dominated by this one plant, but I can assure you, as with all nature, it will find a way to blend in, and before long it will look like it has always been there.

Nostalgia might make me a little biased, but I think there is something quite magical in spring, when little buds burst out of what appeared to be dead wood of deciduous trees, exploding open to reveal beautiful blossom, which a few days later will be alive with our pollinator friends. Once that moment has passed, the nesting birds will soon move in to their treetop hotel and edible fruits will start to appear. All of this life is brought into the garden by just one low-maintenance plant, year after year.

I say low-maintenance because each one of my trees probably only takes about three or four hours of my time each year. Yes, you can get involved with fancy pruning techniques and training your trees to grow in all sorts of fantastic shapes and sizes, but I personally don't. Plus, I don't think the pigeon nesting in my birch tree, the honey bees collecting pollen from my pear tree, or the willow draining excess rainwater in my soil, really care!

Trees are without a doubt the garden's best friend. A garden without a tree is similar to a car without an engine; at a quick glance it may look great, but dig a little deeper and a key component is missing.

If you only take one thing away from this book, please let it be this: pop on your wellies, grab a shovel and plant a tree.

Why are trees so important?

Having touched on why trees are important to me, it is time we talk about a few ways they can help us, our gardens and even our planet – yes, that's right, our planet– they really are that powerful!

Carbon store

Trees have an invisible superpower. They are one of the ultimate carbon capture and storage machines. Trees absorb atmospheric carbon (which is a very good thing) and lock it up for centuries, or until it is felled or burnt. So, let's try to put this into numbers, to explain just how effective they are. A hectare of young woodland with mixed species can capture and lock up over 400 tonnes of carbon!

So how does this all work? Sorry if this gives you flashbacks to school biology classes, but diagrams are the easiest way to explain.

1. By using photosynthesis trees take in carbon and lock it up for years. Atmospheric carbon dioxide is absorbed by the leaves of growing trees, releasing oxygen. This carbon is then locked away until the tree either dies and starts to decay or is destroyed.

   The tree uses sunlight, carbon dioxide and water to make glucose during photosynthesis. Carbon dioxide enters the underside of the leaves via the stomata, where it meets the water carried up the trunk from the roots.

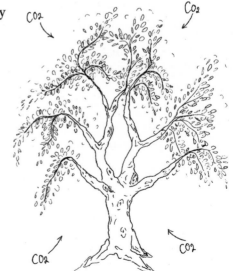

2. When leaves fall from the tree, some of the carbon enters the soil around the floor where it is then also stored.

3. Using the energy from the sunlight a reaction is set off in the leaves between the water and carbon dioxide resulting in glucose, which the tree uses to grow, and oxygen, which is released as a waste product. The carbon ends up in the glucose and helps the tree to grow!

4. The tree now becomes one giant carbon-capturing block, helping to provide a lifeline for so many species, all while helping clean up the carbon dioxide us humans produce!

Trees really are the unsung hero of the garden, just quietly getting on with their job, each individual tree making our world just that little bit better, without us even noticing.

Sometimes all the doom and gloom around global warming can get a little bit depressing and overwhelming. However, politicians and doomsday news outlets fail to mention one thing: we have our own superhero, who can naturally fight this battle against carbon on our behalf – and win!

Giving wildlife a helping hand

I simply cannot think of a single plant, or even habitat, that will provide a safe haven for so many creatures as a tree. You have the obvious wildlife you can see, such as nesting birds, but if you look a little closer you will be surprised at what you might find.

My pear tree is a prime example of just how impactful a small tree in the garden can be for the local wildlife. I spend a lot of time out in the garden– after all, it is my job– and even I am surprised at some of the wildlife I have seen using this tree.

In just the last year I have seen:

* Pigeons nesting in the branches.
* Pollinators feeding from the blossom, including bees, moths and butterflies.
* Bats using the tree as a hunting ground at dusk.
* Squirrels using the tree to move from garden to garden.
* A variety of birds eating the young fruits (as annoying as this might be).
* Mice eating the seeds from the fallen pears.
* Ladybirds using the new branches as a feeding ground.
* Frogs and toads using the shade to escape the punishing summer sun.
* Various beetles and bugs using the trunks as a giant garden highway.

All of this wildlife has been brought into a garden by a medium-size tree I planted with my dad, using the seed from a fallen pear in my primary school garden. I live in the UK, but in other countries there will be many different animal and insect species that will benefit from your trees.

I am lucky enough to have the space for eleven trees and countless shrubs in my garden. Many of my neighbours have as many and some have even more! We live under the Heath-row Airport flight path, however, there is one sound each year that drowns out the noise of jumbo jets flying over. That is all the chirps of baby birds, sat waiting for Mum or Dad to return with a beak full of worms, nesting in the surround-ing trees.

Without a doubt one of the most rewarding feelings is knowing that by planting a few trees and giving them three or four hours of attention a year, you have assisted in bringing so much new life into the world.

For me a garden is a mini ecosystem, but just a tree is a mini ecosystem in its own right. We have all the animals I have spoken about, such as the moths feeding on the pollen, which then provide food for the bats and birds, who provide food for hungry foxes, and on the cycle goes. There is also an often-overlooked world of micro-organisms, fungi and lichens that call trees home, propping up this whole mini world. Even when the leaves fall off the trees in the autumn, they provide a safe haven for mice and hedgehogs, as well as rotting down to improve the soil below. All of this makes trees the ultimate host to many little ecosystems, most of which we will never even know are living there.

MY TOP FIVE TREES FOR WILDLIFE

Cherry: Beautiful early spring blossom brightens up the garden and provides food for pollinators. Once the blossom passes, delicious fruits emerge, providing food for hungry insects, birds and humans.

Chestnut: These large trees provide a safe haven for a vast array of wildlife, as well as producing edible chestnuts, which fall from the tree canopy in the autumn and feed the wildlife below.

Crab apple: These produce fantastic spring blooms, which the local pollinators adore, as well as fruit in autumn for the birds and insects.

Holly: Many varieties of holly are evergreen, giving wildlife precious safe space all year around. Holly can also provide berries for wildlife during the winter, when other food may be scarce.

Rowan: This family of tree will often attract aphids and sawflies, one of the favourite snacks for young birds. The berries are also a real hit.

Grow your own fresh fruit

While trees play a vital role in reducing carbon and helping our local wildlife, for me this is an additional bonus to the main reason I grow them.

The majority of our favourite fruits that we eat are grown on either a tree or a bush. Some of my favourites are pears, plums, apples, cherries, apricots, peaches, nectarines, many types of nuts, figs, avocado, kiwi, oranges, lemons and citrus fruits, olives, coconut, pomegranate, mango, plus so many more! This list could keep going and going, but I think you get the idea.

What may surprise a few people is at for many of these fruit there will be a variety for most climates. Here in the UK many people think you can only grow apples, pears and maybe plums if we are getting really exotic. However, in reality it is far more exciting than that! We grow all of the above– minus coconuts and mangoes –all in a relatively small space in our back garden. The supermarkets are packed with kiwis flown in from New Zealand, oranges from Florida and lemons from Sicily, but maybe we should be thinking a bit closer to home? While kiwis from Berkshire might not have the same ring to it, it would save thousands of food miles each year.

Fresh fruit picked straight from the tree is the best summer treat the garden has to offer, and the pigeons definitely agree! Every year I will be eyeing up that perfect cherry, or think this is the year I will finally make elderberry champagne, only for Mr and Mrs Pigeon to beat me to it! The garden wildlife seems to have the ability to notice the second a fruit is ripe, and just like that it is gone.

While this can be annoying, it shows the tree is doing its job! After all, I have just spent the last two chapters talking about wildlife and rewilding, so it would be hypocritical of me to complain too much.

I am lucky enough to have enough fruit trees to be able to share with the birds and squirrels, but if you only have one or two small fruit trees here are my top five eco-friendly ways you can protect your fruits:

1. Make sure to provide the wildlife in your garden with an alternative food source. Bird feeders filled with seed should help to keep those hungry eyes off your soft fruits.

2. If you are growing dwarf varieties or have an immature tree, you have the benefit of being able to use a net. This is not one hundred per cent effective, as birds will often sit on the net and peck off the outer fruits, but it should protect the fruits in the middle.

3. You can also hang old DVDs, CDs, aluminium tins or anything that has a reflective/shiny surface from the branches. As these blow in the wind, they will start to flash in the sun, helping to divert otherwise hungry mouths to your bird feeders .

4. The most expensive option, but the one I highly recommend, is a fruit cage. These are basically giant nets wrapped around a structure with a door to let you in and out. It saves having to worry about netting each individual small tree one by one.

5. Try making a good old-fashioned scarecrow. Now this one might not be the most effective, but it is the most fun! Use some old clothes, and pack them full of straw, then support your scarecrow with a cane running down the trouser leg into the ground or pot. The straw will also provide a home for all sorts of insects.

Climate control, flood defence and sound barrier

In the last few years, I have really noticed a dramatic change in our weather conditions. In the UK our winters are getting wetter and our summers are getting hotter. Last winter my garden flooded six times between November and February, and in the summer, we had four days over 40°C (104°F)! Around the globe we are seeing record rainfall in some areas, and others are experiencing increased droughts and forest fires. While this can all seem a bit scary, our superhero friend the tree can really help us manage our changing weather conditions.

We all know it is a good idea to try our best to reduce the amount we use our heating in the winter and, for those who have it, air-conditioning in the summer. However, the question is, how can we do this without freezing in the winter or overheating in the summer? The solution, as crazy as it may sound, could be to plant a tree, or two, or maybe three!

So, how do trees help us climate control our homes and gardens? I find two major climate benefits my trees and shrubs offer: the first is summer shade, and the second is a winter wind barrier.

Shade

Deciduous trees – meaning trees that lose their leaves and become dormant in the winter – can produce a lot of shade, especially in the summer months when they are full of leaves. These leaves will help to block direct sunlight beaming down on your home and garden, helping to keep it cool. The beauty of deciduous trees is they start to produce foliage just as we need the shade, and lose their foliage in the winter when the sun on your house is beneficial.

I have strategically planted my trees around the garden to give shade where needed, without posing any risk to the buildings. This includes my garden office and also my driveway, where I park my car. In the summer months this shade helps to keep the interior of my car cool, which reduces the amount of fuel I use to bring the temperature down when I begin a journey.

The leaves on your trees not only help to cast shade, they also release water vapour through transpiration. This helps to keep the surrounding area cool in the summer; paved or concrete areas have no natural way to self-cool. You can experience a great example of this by heading into your local town or city. On a hot summer's day it will always feel warmer than your planted suburb or park only a few miles down the road.

Windbreak

I think the winter benefit of trees is possibly not as valued as the summer shade they provide. This could be due to these benefits not being as visual or the effects not being as immediately noticeable, but they are as important.

In the winter, cooler winds often blow around my home, with draughts finding their way inside the house via the cracks in the windows and the doors, causing me to turn up the heating. By planting a row of evergreens in the direction of my prevailing wind, I have created a natural wind block, helping to reduce the cold wind blowing against the house. It is important to also remember that evergreens can block our precious winter sunlight, so please make sure to factor this in to your planting. Planting a deciduous tree is a great way to remove any risk of blocking out all the winter sun, while also helping to block out some cold winter wind.

A bonus of planting a winter windbreak is it can also double up as a natural sound barrier. Since the natural calm of the Covid lockdowns, I have really noticed just how loud modern life has become. The droning sound of car tyres on the roads, the seemingly endless construction noise and the bellowing from air traffic flying overhead have unfortunately become part of life. A row of trees or shrubs will block out a surprising amount of this noise pollution, allowing you to enjoy your natural space in relative peace.

Flood defence

As already mentioned, recently we have experienced quite a lot of flooding in my area due to extreme rainfall, and this extreme weather only seem to be getting more regular. In the last ten years my garden has flooded ten times – nine of which have happened in the last two years! I have noticed that in the area where my trees are planted the flooding is dramatically less than in the open exposed parts of the garden.

When I am out and about and it starts to rain, I often seek cover under the nearest tree. This is because the branches and canopy will stop a lot of the rainfall from ever reaching the floor below. This same effect is really important in our gardens. The summer tree-top canopy really helps to spread the rainfall over a longer period of time, as it catches and holds a large amount of the water. Some of this rainfall will evaporate from the tree and never reach the ground. By spreading out the levels of rain that hit the ground at one time, it also gives the surface water a chance to penetrate before the ground becomes waterlogged. This dramatically reduces the level of surface water runoff. Any water that does make it through the tree-top canopy to the floor will have an easier time penetrating through the soil, due to the tree's root system. This means the water will not puddle on the surface, causing a large amount of runoff, which leads to flooding. The theory sounds great, and I do really notice the reduced levels of flooding in my garden. The areas under the fruit orchard and willow trees never flood, whereas the open lawn or paved patio seem to flood multiple times every year now!

The Woodland Trust estimates that in the UK alone flood prevention provided by trees is worth around £6.5 billion! By all of us planting a tree or two, hopefully we can continue to bring this number up and up.

What tree can I plant in my space?

We all have different-size gardens, and some people may be thinking, no way do I have space for a tree! However, trust me, there really is a tree for all shapes and sizes of garden. With a bit of careful planning and advice, even a balcony can be a great place for a tree. Before we get too carried away with what varieties to go out and buy and how to plant your new tree, let's establish what size space you have first.

For me, it is easy to think about gardens in five categories:

1. Small balcony/courtyard – Up to 9 sq metres (100 sq feet)

2. Large balcony/small garden – Up to 59 sq metres (600 sq feet)

3. Medium garden – Up to 230 sq metres (2,500 sq feet)

4. Large garden – Up to half a hectare (1 acre)

5. Country garden – Anything over half a hectare or 1(1acre). This is quite rare, but I like to use this as my dream scenario, where I can imagine my fantasy garden.

Once you have identified the size of your garden, this is where the fun really starts. I have compiled a list of my top five tree picks for each size space, but it is always a good idea to speak to your local tree nursery to see what is best for your local area. A good plant nursery will love to have a chat and help you select the best tree for your needs.

Small balcony/courtyard

With a small balcony space is obviously very limited and you will need to consider the weight limitations, too. But don't let that put you off, as there are plenty of amazing trees you can grow in pots. It is also worth keeping your tree well pruned. I love to let my plants go wild but in a small space you want room to move without having to traverse branches and leaves everywhere. A lot of trees will have a dwarf variety rootstock available, so please make sure you are selecting these for your balcony, otherwise in a few years you may have a few issues.

My top five picks are:

1. Olive

2. Japanese maple (Acer)

3. A well pruned bay laurel

4. Citrus (which can be moved inside during the winter to make a fantastic large houseplant, just please keep that in mind as you will need room inside too).

5. Dwarf peach tree

Large balcony/small garden

With this size of space you are still realistically planting your trees in large pots. However, there is a lot more scope than with a small balcony. It is still a good idea to buy dwarf varieties and keep up with pruning, as many trees will soon take over a small space, leaving you with nothing but shade in your garden. All the trees in the above section will be great, but my top five picks are:

1. Dwarf apple tree

2. Dwarf pear tree

3. Fig

4. Dwarf cherry

5. Small magnolia

Medium garden

Chances are that with this amount of space you will be growing your tree out in the ground rather than in a container. This opens up a whole new world of trees and varieties that would just be too demanding or big to keep in a pot. As before, all of the trees mentioned above will work, but my top five picks are:

1. Japanese dogwood

2. Hawthorn

3. Crab apple

4. Rowan

5. Hardy palm tree

Large garden

If you are lucky enough to have a large garden, then you are spoilt for choice. I have a decent-sized garden and I like to mix it up with smaller and larger trees. Some of my trees, like the citrus varieties, are grown in pots, as I like to move them around and bring them inside during winter, and others are grown in the ground to reach their full size. All of the trees mentioned above will work, but my top five picks are:

1. Silver birch

2. Elder

3. Hazel

4. Willow

5. Oak

Country garden

I like to class anything over half a hectare (an acre) as a country garden, and if you are lucky enough to have a garden this big then you really are spoilt for choice. I would recommend a section of flowering trees such as magnolia as well as an orchard of fruit trees. If I had a space this large, I would also go wild with a few of nature's giant varieties, such as oak and redwood. In a garden this size you can really let your imagination run wild, and pretty much any tree you can think of will happily fit.

My top five picks are:

1. Douglas fir

2. Giant sequoia

3. Norway spruce

4. Yew

5. Chestnut

All of my top picks are just suggestions of what I would plant in my UK climate. As I mentioned earlier, it is always best for you to let your imagination run wild then let your local nursery advise you for your specific area. I would love to have a mango, jackfruit and coconut tree, but in my climate it simply isn't possible.

The main takeaway here is, no matter where you live and what size space you have available, there will be a tree to enhance your garden and benefit you, nature and our planet.

Okay, enough talking about trees and how amazing they are, now let's have some fun and get planting. Planting trees could not be easier, and I have a few tips up my sleeve to make sure both you and your tree are as happy as possible. The basic fundamentals are the same whether you are planting in a pot or in open ground, but it is worth talking about each one independently as there are a few differences.

I have always maintained that I am not a plant expert, however, I am addicted to reading gardening books and other literature and then applying what I have read in practice, and tweaking it to find my own style that works. I have been doing this almost since the day I could read, as well as being outside getting my hands dirty in the garden with my great-grandmother before that, successfully growing trees in pots and the ground. The great part about trees is the proof is in the pudding because they live for many years. These are my methods of planting, but that doesn't mean they are the only ones.

My quick guide to planting and growing your tree in a pot

Growing trees in pots is very easy and can add blossom, fruit,shade, privacy and nature to a small area. Even though I have the space to plant out in the garden, using pots is my favourite way to grow lots of my trees. I love having the ability to move them around to different locations and protect them in the colder months by bringing them into the conservatory as house plants. Having said that, growing trees in pots is more demanding and challenging than in open ground. But by following these steps, I have all the faith that your potted tree will be a success!

What you need:

* A deep pot, at least 45 cm (18 in) wide at the top, but ideally the bigger the better.
* A good soil-based compost; I would avoid multipurpose compost as it will dry out too fast.
* Your chosen tree, making sure it is a dwarf variety or is suitable for a pot, such as citrus, olive or any others mentioned in the small balcony or courtyard recommendations (see page 221).
* A tree stake and tree tie.
* Controlled-release plant food, to be administered throughout the spring and summer months.
* Watering can and enough water to fill it up a few times.
* Rocks or a broken terracotta pot.

Container options

PLASTIC

Plastic pots work well and are affordable, and currently my cherry tree is growing in a large plastic pot. The downside to cheap plastic pots is they can be damaging to the environment, and may not give you any longevity as the sun can make them brittle.

TERRACOTTA

In my opinion these are the best pots to use in the garden. They look great and due to the porous nature of terracotta, they let air and moisture in and out, assisting root development. However, sometimes trees in terracotta pots will dry out too fast and struggle to retain enough moisture. If looked after, a terracotta pot will last a lifetime, but be warned, they can suffer quite bad frost damage in a cold winter.

WOOD

Wooden containers look amazing but can get very expensive. It is also worth having a look to check if the wood has been treated. Wooden pots tend to look great when they are new, but age fast and are prone to rot.

METAL

I am cautious about recommending any metal pots and especially not for trees. In the summer months they cause the soil to heat up to unbearable temperatures, making your already tricky task of watering even harder, with the reverse problem in the winter.

My personal choice would have to be either terracotta or a really good plastic pot. What is arguably more important is that the top of the pot must not be narrower than the bottom or middle of the pot, as this makes it very hard to transplant your tree once it outgrows that pot.

Before we get too carried away with planting, I have a little check-list you might want to use when buying a tree. Most of the trees we buy are containerized, so it is a good idea to check the roots. A good plant nursery will never object to you popping the tree out of its pot, so you can check the roots. If the tree does not want to separate from the pot, it is most likely rootbound, and it is best to leave that one. Alternatively, you may pop it out of the pot and there are no roots visible, which could mean the tree is not well established. You are looking for a few roots at the bottom of the pot, without them going around and around in circles.

Now we have our tools, pot and tree, let's get planting!

Step-by-step guide to planting your tree in a pot

STEP 1:

Start with a large pot, making sure the top of the pot is at least as wide as the bottom. Place a few stones or bits of broken terracotta around the drainage hole to stop it getting blocked, and fill up the bottom of your pot with a good soil-based compost.

STEP 2:

Remove your tree from the small pot it was in when your purchased it and place into the larger pot, making sure the top of the roots are all the way in, and the thick part of the trunk is just above the top of the pot. If the roots of your tree are tightly packed together, gently tease a few of the outer and bottom roots apart. Once your tree is in, fill up the rest of the pot with your soil, giving the tree a little wiggle as you do so to avoid any major air pockets.

STEP 3:

Water your new tree really well, making sure the water has reached all the available soil, and not just run down the side of the pot and out the drainage holes. Continue to check your tree every other day, making sure it has enough water. A good way to tell if your tree needs a drink is to dig a little way into the soil with your hands. If the soil feels dry after about 7 cm (3 in), then give your tree a drink.

STEP 4:

Insert your tree stake into the pot, being careful of any roots, and once it is secure, fasten the tree to the stake with a rubber tree tie. It is important to make sure the tree tie is not fastened too tight as that will damage the tree as it grows. Alternatively, you can even use a more robust support system for more challenging trees, as seen in the illustration.

Top tip

Bury a smaller pot with drainage holes, with the top of the pot being level with the top of the surrounding soil, in your larger pot. You can then water directly into this smaller pot, and the water will run out the drainage holes and go straight into the soil surrounding the roots.

My quick guide to planting and growing your tree in open ground

Planting your tree directly out in the garden is arguably much easier than in a pot, and it will require less attention. Just remember, it is very hard to move a tree once it is settled in the garden. Take your time and plan where you want it to grow, thinking about buildings, structures and shade. It is highly likely the tree you plant will outlive you, so it is important we get it off to a good start.

What you need:

* Your chosen tree, making sure it is well established but not root bound.
* A tree stake and tree tie.
* Controlled-release plant food, to be administered throughout the spring and summer months.
* Watering can and enough water to fill it up a few times.
* A good spade and fork and maybe some gardening gloves.

Step-by-step guide to planting your tree in the garden

STEP 1:

When planting out in the garden, it is vital you prepare your planting position. My favourite way to do this is to fork over a wide area of soil the depth of the root ball. This will help aerate the soil and stop it from easily getting waterlogged. When doing this I add in a good amount of compost, but avoid manure at this stage.

STEP 2:

Remove the tree from the pot and dig a hole at least four times the diameter of the root ball and the same depth as the root ball. Place your root ball in the middle of the hole and gently tease out a few roots to spread them across.

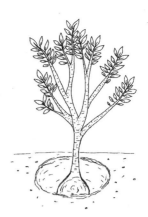

STEP 3:

Backfill the soil into the hole all around the root ball. It is a good idea to gently shake the tree as you do this, to make sure the soil falls around the roots, and helping to avoid air pockets forming. The very top of the root ball should be just underneath the original soil level.

STEP 4:

Place your tree stake next to your tree, being careful not to hit any roots. If your tree is secure in a sheltered position, you can skip this. Secure your tree to the stake using a rubber tree tie, making sure to loosen it as the trunk grows. Water your tree really well and check if it needs a drink every other day for the first week or two.

Good news story

Brazilian husband and wife team, helping to restore the country's forests!

Brazilian photographer Sebastião Salgado and wife Lélia have taken planting trees in their garden to a whole new level! The husband-and-wife team have spent the last 20 years restoring more than 700 hectares (1,750 acres) of barren land back into dense forests, packed with all sorts of flora and fauna.

After covering the Rwandan genocide, Salgado returned to his family's former cattle ranch to find a lifeless patch of land. Saddened by what they saw, they decided to get to work.

With the help of other locals, the couple have got to work planting millions of trees and plants. This project slowly brought the area back to life. Now more than 300 hundred species of trees, over 170 species of birds, 30 mammal and 15 amphibian species, call the farm home.

This restoration project has been so successful it is now a federally recognized nature reserve. Millions of new tree saplings are now raised on the ranch, and they provide training and support for local farmers too.

Taking care of your tree

Now your tree is planted it is important to remember it is very much as alive as the birds and insects using it as a safe haven. It can be easy to get lost with tree care, because it can be quite a tricky topic that takes years to learn. I will share my little checklist I use to keep my trees happy and healthy. It may seem like a lot, but attending each one only takes around three to four hours of my time annually.

My quick-reference tree-care checklist:

* **Weather damage:** After any extreme weather, it is worth checking your tree's branches for damage. Locate any damaged branches and safely remove to avoid them falling and causing any further damage.

* **Check tree ties:** Tree ties left unchecked will soon restrict growing trunks, causing damage to the tree. Check regularly and loosen when needed.

* **Check tree stakes:** Tree stakes are useful while your tree is young, but once your tree is established it is good to let it grow naturally on its own. Give your tree a gentle wiggle, and if there is lots of movement leave the stake; if the tree seems sturdy, it is time to remove the stake.

* **Check for any signs of disease:** There are a range of diseases that can affect your trees, but luckily quite a few are treatable. It is a good idea to regularly check the bark, trunk and leaves for any abnormalities. If things do not look quite right, check in with your local tree surgeon.

* **Watering:** From experience, the number one cause of young trees and potted trees running into issues is lack of water. In the warmer months, which in my UK climate is April to October, check your trees at least once a week to see if they need a

good drink. I like to dig in with my hand to feel the soil a little way below the surface. If it feels dry, give your tree a big drink, which for me is at least a large full watering can, but if you think it needs more than don't be afraid to give it more.

* **Feed your tree:** It is a good idea to feed your tree each year. There are a few ways you can do this, but my favourite is to add new organic compost around the base.

* **Check your potted trees:** If you have planted your tree in a pot, every year you will need to check to see if you need to pot it on into a larger pot. I normally upsize my pots every other year.

* **Pruning:** While I like to let my trees go wild, if you are growing in a smaller area it is a good idea to give your tree an annual haircut. Pruning trees can be quite a science depending on seasons and the variety. You can find a lot of information about each pruning style in books or online, or better still, seek advice from your local tree surgeon.

* **Check for signs of life:** Sometimes when a branch or a tree appears to be dead, it can actually still be very much alive. A good way to test is to gently scratch the surface, and if under the bark is still green, then it is alive.

* **Check for any wildlife:** Before doing any major work to your tree, please check for any signs of wildlife. Always check for nests in the branches and small mammals living in fallen leaves or twigs under the tree.

* **Mulch:** Each year I like to add a good layer of mulch around the base of any young tree. This will help lock in moisture and will reduce your need to water during the dry months.

This is my basic checklist; tree care is a very complex subject and can be quite dangerous. Always take care when removing large parts of trees or climbing into them. I recommend seeking professional help for any major jobs.

My dos and don'ts of growing trees

✓ Grow dwarf or small trees in pots

✓ Carry out regular health checks on your tree

✓ Water young trees regularly

✓ Plant your potted plants in containers with a diameter larger at the top than the bottom, to help with transplanting

✓ Feed your trees each year

✓ Plant in a peat-free soil-based compost

✓ Check the roots of your potted trees before buying

✓ Plant at the correct time

✓ Encourage wildlife to use trees

DON'T

✗ Plant your tree near buildings or structures such as fences. As a general rule I will leave at least double the amount of room it needs ; so for instance,if a bush has a spread of 3 metres (10 feet), I would leave 6 (20)!

✗ Grow large trees in a small space

✗ Plant in multipurpose compost

✗ Plant in metal pots

✗ Buy without checking the root health of the tree

✗ Leave the tree in the small pot you bought it in from the store

✗ Bury the root ball too deep when planting out

✗ Trample the dug soil after planting

✗ Over-fertilize with manure

Now the hard work is done, it is time to sit back and enjoy the fruits of your labour, if you will pardon the pun.

Checklist

Have your notebook and pencil handy to make a note of your answers to the following prompts:

→ What tree have you planted?

→ What is your favourite bird you have seen on your tree?

→ What tree do you want to plant next?

→ Have you given your tree a name?

→ How much has your tree grown in the last six months?

→ Write a list of all the wildlife you have seen using your tree.

→ Have you encountered any issues during your monthly checks?

My NHS:
The Natural
Health System

Health is wealth, so the saying goes, and I could not agree more. So far, we have explored quite a few ways we can use our gardens to help nature and our planet, but none of this is possible without first prioritizing our own health and wellbeing.

I should probably begin by explaining what I mean by NHS. Where I live, in the UK, the National Health Service refers to the publicly funded healthcare systems in England, Scotland, Northern Ireland and Wales. However, for me there is another NHS. One we can all access, no matter where in the world we live, and that is my NHS: the Natural Health System.

A few years ago, I injured my back and could not move without severe pain. As anyone who has badly hurt their back knows, the pain is debilitating, and I was confined to my bed for five days straight. This just so happened to be around Christmas time, too – a time of year I normally love, but that year was different. I did not care about Christmas; I did not care about presents, or any other festivities for that matter! All I could think about was getting better, and wishing for a miracle cure. It consumed me, not just the physical side of the pain but the mental side too.

Fortunately, I recovered quite fast, but that feeling has stayed with me, and I believe it will stay with me for the rest of my life. It certainly was the wake-up call I needed to start taking my health a little more seriously, and for me the garden has been my saving grace, both physically and mentally.

Currently there are multiple studies being conducted, looking into the relationship between gardening and our overall health. There seems to be consistent consensus: gardening has a positive impact on our mental and physical health. This is fantastic news, but most gardeners could have told them that! For me the unanswered question I would like to explore is why?

Now in much the same way that I am not a horticultural or botanical expert, I am also not an expert on human health, nor do I have a large body of research to prove any points. What I do have is a lifetime's experience of what gardening has done for me, as well as a nearly two-million people strong online family, who share their experiences and thoughts with me too.

I strongly believe the garden, gardening and being outside in nature is the secret key to a happy and healthy life. After all, when the world shut down due to Covid, those of us lucky enough to have a garden all of a sudden noticed this fantastic plot of land just outside our door. Those without a garden also turned to parks and green spaces for a sense of calm and salvation during a crazy time.

So next time you are feeling a little bit unhealthy or slightly down, I recommend popping those gardening shoes back on and heading out into the fresh air of our gardens and outside spaces. The natural health system has worked wonders for me and many others, and I hope it will work for you too!

Gardening for physical health

By now we all know that getting up off the sofa and exercising is generally a good idea. It helps to keep us physically fit, mobile and can reduce the chances of many health complications, such as heart disease and type 2 diabetes. The older I get, the more I am starting to appreciate just how important exercising can be. No longer can I eat what I want and stay in shape, or be as sprightly as I once was without putting in some effort. That effort does not have to be a chore, though. That is the wonderful part about utilizing our gardens and outside spaces: while it is fantastic exercise, it rarely feels like a chore!

As the years have rolled on, I have found consistently going to the gym and following a fitness routine is simply not as easy as it was when I had the flexibility that being at university offered. After a busy day at work, the last thing most people want is to do is battle through a crowded weights section, wait for a treadmill to become available or be exposed to all the general noise and chaos of a gym. So, like so many others, my gym habit soon fell away once I started full-time work.

A few years ago, I was in the garden digging out weeds and just generally plodding around doing bits and pieces, very proudly wearing my new smart watch for the first time. After around an hour or so, I looked down to check the time and got a shock! I had burned 350 calories and kept my heart rate in the zone generally accepted as a healthy elevated position for over an hour. The penny dropped; from that moment the garden has become my new gym! Now, I have mentioned calories burnt as an indicator and to help paint a picture, but what is more important is I felt fantastic! It did not feel like a chore, neither did I feel taxed or worn out. Instead, I was more surprised and inspired, it gave me another reason to get outside in nature even more; not that I needed any more reasons too!

While gardening, my mind is busy on whatever job I am doing. This could be weeding, digging, planting, carrying, or any other garden job. At no point am I ever really thinking about the movement or the exercise itself. I believe this is why gardening as a tool for exercise can be so powerful. I can exercise for a longer period of time, and burn a lot of calories, compared to say going for a jog, where you are actively focusing on the movement and exercise. Plus, gardening allows me to get jobs done while exercising at the same time, which is good for you, good for your garden and also very enjoyable, which is a win in my books! I would like to add, it does not need to just be jobs around your garden; if you have a very small garden or balcony, you may soon run out of jobs to do. Try to instead think broader, is there a local wood you can go foraging in, for example? When foraging, please make sure to check local laws as to where you can and cannot gather, as well as do thorough research to make sure what you have found is safe to eat. Never consume anything you are unsure about.

Gardening allows you to use muscles you might not use in standard daily life, and as a result build up a lot more strength, without necessarily realizing. A slightly worrying fact is that from the age of thirty, our bodies can start to lose muscle, so it is important we try to take some steps to limit this. As you know, I have been gardening all my life, so when at the age of eighteen my friends and I joined the gym, I was noticeably stronger than them. I like to refer to this as farm strength. Years of carrying heavy bags of compost and moving large pots about naturally built up my strength over time, but in a far less direct and aggressive way than going and lifting weights.

A great example of farm strength can be seen on almost any allotment. Watch and compare the physical abilities and flexibility of some of the more mature members, who have likely been gardening for years, with another average person of a similar age. The results might shock and impress you. John, who has the allotment opposite me, is in his eighties. I regularly see him lifting bags of compost and wheeling heavy wheelbarrows around the plot with relative ease! My great-grandmother, who gardened her whole life, would put many younger people to shame when it came to lifting, shovelling and bending, even when she was in her early nineties! If you compare John and my great-grandmother to people of a similar age, who have led a more sedentary lifestyle, you will often see stark differences.

To expand my research on this topic, I have been doing different garden tasks over the last year with my smart watch on, and tracking the calories burned to take an average, as well as monitoring how I feel physically too. Some of these may surprise you, but please remember these figures are only a record of my experience, and are also relevant to my body size, shape and age and will most likely be different to yours. Please remember, physical fitness is not all about calories burnt, but rather how you feel before, during and after. The goal should never solely be to burn as many calories as possible, but rather to find a nice balance, where you feel good within your own body, and week by week you may start to notice improvements to aspects of your physical health, such as flexibility and stamina. With that said, calories help me showcase the physical benefits of gardening, so here are some of the more interesting results of doing 30 minutes of activity on some different garden tasks::

* digging soil – 250 calories burned

* mowing lawn – 180 calories burned

* watering with watering cans – 135 calories burned

* pruning branches – 138 calories burned

* wheelbarrowing and shovelling woodchip – 230 calories burned

* planting potatoes – 196 calories burned

* sowing seeds – 110 calories burned

* harvesting – 130 calories burned

* mulching – 190 calories burned

* planting out seedlings – 125 calories burned

* cleaning out the pond – 153 calories burned

* painting the shed and fences – 139 calories burned

* washing the greenhouse glass – 123 calories burned

* general garden tidy up – 145 calories burned

Obviously, this is only energy used and does not take into account the different muscles that have been worked, and many other factors, but I found it interesting none the less. It is clear gardening can have very similar benefits to traditional forms of exercise, while in my admittedly biased opinion, be a lot more fun. It is also worth noting these tasks were also completed at my usual leisurely pace, and I did not make any extra effort to boost the scores.

There is a very important reason why each task was only thirty minutes long. Gardening jobs regularly involve a lot of repeated motions. If you start a big garden task and continue to do that one job until it is finished, chances are the next morning you will have a sharp reminder of the previous day's activities, due to repetitive strain. The easiest way I have found to decrease this pain is to simply alternate jobs and change position regularly. After all, you would not go to the gym and bench press for three hours straight, and the same applies to your gardening jobs.

These numbers also highlight just how physical gardening can be. I think it is important to touch on how vital it is to stay hydrated and take regular breaks, and it probably explains why many people keep a tin of biscuits and a kettle in the shed (or that might just be my excuse for my hidden tin of biscuits!).

Stretching

This may sound a little bit odd, but before any big gardening/foraging session, I like to stretch for ten minutes or so. It is normal to stretch for any form of traditional exercise, so why not gardening? I will admit, it can be a little bit embarrassing stretching outside in the garden or at the allotment, so I normally do this in the privacy of my own home.

A simple ten-minute basic stretching routine will allow you to accomplish more in each gardening session, while also reducing the risks of any injuries. Since I have incorporated stretching before each session, I have not sustained any injuries or niggles, whereas before, when I was getting stuck into the garden without stretching, I always had an underlying injury somewhere.

Stretching really does not have to be complex or advanced. I use a really basic, beginner-friendly ten-minute stretching routine. I do these six simple stretches before any long session in the garden, but please remember that these are only a guide, and it is always wise to use stretches that are suitable for your ability:

1. Cobra stretch – do 8 repetitions

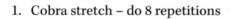

2. Knee-to-chest – hold each knee for 45 second

3. Shoulder stretch – hold each arm for 45 seconds

4. Hamstring stretch – hold each leg for 45 seconds

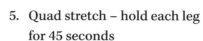

5. Quad stretch – hold each leg for 45 seconds

6. Side stretch – 10 repetitions each side

As you start to become accustomed to the idea of stretching, and seeing how your body starts to respond to each stretch, I recommend designing your own routine. Trying lots of different stretches will help you figure out what works the best for you. I would also like to add that while during the summer months the stretching helped, he effect was far more noticeable during the cooler winter months . So please, on a cooler day, take a little bit more time to warm up and stretch. I would also like to add I do not stretch each and every time I am going to do a little bit of gardening. If I'm heading outside to water a few of my container plants, for example, this isn't really necessary, however, if I am planning on digging up my potato rows at the allotment, then I would always consider having a little stretch.

My example garden fitness plan; how to get more exercise in the garden.

It is all well and good talking about my experiences, but let's now have a look how you might be able to apply gardening for physical health in practice at home.

Depending on my energy levels or if I am gardening for exercise or just to get the jobs done, I would start by thinking about the tools I would use for each job. Do I want speed and ease, or do I want to have a bit more of a manual experience, which will be more exercise. Gardening can be as physically demanding as you may or may not want it to be. I will admit some days I quite like an easy life and will use all the tools at my disposal to just make it that little bit easier, whereas on other days I might be feeling up for a bit more of a challenge!

For example:

Watering: Watering can vs hosepipe

Pruning/trimming: Hand saw vs hand clippers vs power saw

Mowing lawn: Push lawn mower vs petrol or electric mower

Moving compost bags: Carry individually vs loading into wheelbarrow

Cleaning pathways: Hand washing vs pressure washer

Foraging: Walking to the woods or foraging spot vs driving there

As with everything in this book, please be aware that some options may also be slightly more eco-friendly than others. For example, not only are hand tools and watering cans better for your physical health, but they are also a more eco-conscious choice than power tools and hose pipes.

Staying safe in the garden

Gardening is as hard or as easy as you would like to make it for yourself, but it is also important to remember your limitations. That 30-metre (100-foot) flower border you want to dig may seem like a great idea, but the task may be too big to do on your own. Trust me, I have bitten off more than I can chew in the garden quite a few times.

Gardening is fun and rewarding, and as a result it is easy to get carried away and overdo it. Far easier than in the gym or traditional exercise, as you are not aware of just how much exercise you are doing. I have often taken on too much, especially on a hot sunny day, where you are stuck into a task, enjoying the sun and then when you go back inside you realize you are dehydrated, sunburnt and exhausted.

I have put together a little checklist I like to use, just as a reminder to myself to stay safe and not to get too carried away:

* **Mobile phone:** It is always a good idea to keep your mobile phone on you while gardening, especially if you are on your own. If you find yourself in trouble, you can call or message someone for help, or alternatively, in serious situations, you can call emergency services.

* **Water:** I like to keep a few bottles of fresh water in my garden shed. During the hot summer months, it is so easy to get carried away in the garden and forget to drink!

* **Appropriate shoes:** Garden clogs and flip flops are great if you are just out enjoying the garden, but for any actual gardening jobs, I would always recommend enclosed shoes or boots.

* **Sun cream:** Even during cloudy days we still need some protection from the sun's UV rays, I keep a good bottle of sun cream next to my tools in the shed as a reminder to use it.

* **Do not overdo it:** As I mentioned earlier it is very easy to get carried away in the garden and do a little bit too much. Take regular breaks and divide large jobs into smaller, manageable sections.

* **Gloves:** I always wear gloves while undertaking heavy garden work such as digging, or handling any tricky plants such as nettles and brambles. It is surprising how fast your hands can blister when digging or raking, and there are plenty of plants that want to sting, stab and poke you. A good pair of gloves will help to prevent all of this.

* **Avoid prolonged repetitive motions:** A lot of gardening jobs involve repetitive motions, which can easily cause repetitive strain. I like to rotate repetitive jobs every thirty minutes.

* **Right tool for the right job:** I have tried to use the wrong tool for the job a few times, one I am guilty of all the time is pruning large branches with small secateurs. The blade often slips, and I have had some close shaves, if you pardon the pun.

* **First aid box:** In my shed there is a full first aid kit, luckily, I have never needed to use it, but it is there ready in the case of an emergency.

* **Clean sharp tools:** I find sharp tools never slip as you rarely have to apply too much pressure on the tool.

* **Protect your eyes:** Gardening involves a lot of bending and crouching down. Please be aware of any canes or branches that can poke your eyes. I pop old yoghurt pots on the top of all my bamboo supporting canes to stop them catching my eyes or face as I work on my plants.

The consumer product safety commission reported that emergency rooms in the USA treat over 400,000 garden tool-related injuries per year on average, so please be careful.

Adding more fresh produce to your diet

Exercise is only one area of physical health our gardens can help with; another equally important area is diet. Over the last few years, the message from health care professionals has been pretty clear, we should be incorporating fresh fruits and vegetables into our diet, where possible. Earlier we explored how you can grow your own groceries, no matter how much space you have available. If you use your garden to grow a few crops, naturally you will start to incorporate more into your diet. In the summer months, I regularly head down to the garden to pick a fresh tomato off the vine as a snack and the same can be said for peas, carrots, soft fruits and so many more crops. It would be very unlikely I would have a bowl of store-bought tomatoes, for example, in the kitchen waiting for me to snack on in the same way.

The fantastic part about homegrown food is you will probably start to view your vegetables completely differently to ones you buy in the store. After a few months of caring for the plant and watching it grow, excitement starts to build around the idea of finally eating it. Personally, I find myself planning my meals around whatever vegetable is ready to harvest, whereas when I am buying food in the store, it is easy to prioritize the protein and view the vegetables as a secondary addition to the meal.

If you are anything like me, sometimes you will head to the shops, buy some fresh salad ingredients such as cucumbers, tomatoes and lettuce, only for them to live in the bottom of the fridge where they will most likely rot. I cannot think of a time I have ever let any fresh homegrown produce go to waste. Too much time and energy has gone into growing them, so as soon as they are ready, we will find a way to use them, unconsciously increasing our intake of fresh vegetables.

In so many countries, and especially in the UK, the quality of the 'fresh' produce section is average at best. I am not surprised so many people buy them only for them to go to waste or just snub the vegetables all together. Call me biased, but so many homegrown veggies taste unrecognizably different from their store-bought counterparts. The sense of achievement you get from growing the crops you eat definitely helps with the taste, but there a few more measurable reasons why the store-bought crops may not be as nice. In the Western world we are at risk of falling into the habit of eating food out of season or ripen-at-home crops, due to year-round availability in the supermarkets. By growing your own food at home not only will it help you to eat more fresh food, it also educates you about when certain produce will be in season in the shops too! By learning when produce is in season through growing it yourself, this will also help teach you what is also in season at the supermarket and how to pick the best food on offer there too.

Many vegetables are still developing flavour as they ripen on the plant. Once they are harvested this process often comes to a halt. While they may look ripe on the outside, they can be far from fully

developed vegetables and fruits, lacking in many key flavours. For some crops, such as sweetcorn, once they are harvested their natural sugars start to turn to starch, reducing the sweet flavour. This process can happen quite fast, and by the time the crops reach the store, that lovely sweet and fresh flavour has all but gone.

My little vegetable patch in the garden is my natural multi-vitamin, especially during the summer months. I get my vitamin C from the citrus fruits, vitamin D from the sunshine, and vitamins A and B from most of the other vegetables.

Vitamin D

Vitamin D helps the body regulate its levels of calcium and phosphate. If you have a lack of vitamin D this can lead to bone pain in adults and rickets in children. By getting out in the garden for a few hours each week, especially during the spring and summer months, your body should be able to make all the vitamin D it needs. You cannot overdose on vitamin D from sunlight, but please be careful. Sun cream is always a must, and on very sunny days I recommend a hat too. Anyone who follows me on social media knows, I am never without my straw hat in the garden.

Gardening for wellbeing

We are now starting to think about physical and mental health as equals. I fully support this change, as modern life can be really taxing on our mental health at times. However, could the answer to improving our mental wellbeing be right outside our back door?

I have always known being outside in the garden improves my mood and relaxes my mind. The annoying part is, I cannot tell you one definitive reason why. Could it be happy memories from my childhood? Possibly. Could it be the relaxing sound of the bird call? Maybe. Is it the sense of calm and peace from being surrounded by nature? Perhaps. In truth I believe it is all of these reasons and quite a few more. The garden, and specifically my vegetable patch, has a unique ability to remove whatever stress or anxiety I may be feeling, even if it is only momentarily, as it is a lovely break from reality.

Without even realizing, if I am feeling a bit low, I always end up pottering around in the garden. It happens automatically. One minute I am sat inside feeling sorry for myself, and the next, I am outside weeding, smelling flowers and watering the plants. It is like my brain is wired to tell my legs that's where I need to be during those moments.

When my great-grandmother passed away it hit me hard. It was the first death of a close relative, when I was an age to understand what was happening. I was eighteen at the time, and she was not only my great-grandmother but my best friend and the person who introduced me to gardening. I remember after the funeral was the lowest I have ever felt. I spent that whole evening and pretty much every evening for the next month outside in the garden, alone, just me and my plants. It relaxed my mind and calmed me, gave me a sense of purpose and in a way offered a welcome distraction. Later that same year one of my good friends tragically passed away. The garden helped me through that process too, in much the same way. From then on. I knew, if the garden could help me through these most challenging times, it could help with anything.

How can the garden help with the stress and anxiety of modern life?

If we think about it, most of our stress and anxiety is caused by our thoughts; often thoughts that we have self-fabricated and are normally worse in our heads than reality. Trust me, I fully understand, as I am a massive overthinker myself. For me, the solution is to find an off switch, and the garden is the best one I have found yet.

So how does the garden help me do this? As I mentioned earlier, I cannot pinpoint one specific reason, but rather instead I have identified four key reasons which all help contribute together. There is a lot of research in this area, which is important, but when it comes to mental wellbeing, I strongly believe it is very individualistic and personal. As a result, use the following as a guide, but experiment and find your own additional reasons too.

GET LOST IN THE GARDEN, NOT YOUR THOUGHTS

Most jobs in the garden do not take much thought or reason. You can just naturally chip away, without having to concentrate too hard. If you are stressed or anxious, being alone with your thoughts often allows you to overthink even more. While the jobs do not take much thought, your mind is occupied with the task at hand, preventing your brain from drifting back to negative thoughts. Instead, you can replace these thoughts and get lost in the joys of nature and the natural world.

EXPRESS YOURSELF

Getting out in the garden is your chance to go wild and get creative. Think outside the box and think big! If you fail, who cares; if something does not quite work the first time, try again. There are so many external factors to gardening, even the experts do not get everything right all the time, I mean, I have multiple fails each and every year too! That is the fabulous part about your garden, it is just you, and nobody to impress. Try to focus on the process more than the result, plus in many climates, once winter arrives it will wipe your slate virtually clean, and you can start fresh the following spring. By having a fun project to work on at home, it gives you more purpose in your free time, and a sense of achievement when it is completed, which is elevated further if it is a success.

PHYSICAL BENEFITS

We have just explored the ways gardening can help keep you fit, but exercise can also make you feel good mentally. When we get up and get active, our heart rate increases, which pumps blood to the brain, and can increase endorphins and serotonin levels, these are the brain chemicals that make us feel good.

SENSE OF ACHIEVEMENT

In a way, a gardener is similar to a conductor and their orchestra, making sure each instrument comes into play at the correct time, but then stepping back and letting each musician have control over that instrument. Gardeners have to do the same, by getting their plants started, then let nature take over, and just every now and again make sure it is playing to the right tune, and make amendments where necessary. On the whole gardening is easy. Plants want to grow; it is down to us to not get in their way. I promise, you will have far more successes with your garden than fails, and remember that every single gardener will fail with something, each and every year. There is something magical about bringing fresh new life into the world, and that is what you are achieving with your plants.

It is important to remember gardening is not about achieving perfection. A mouse is going to dig up your seeds, a slug is going to eat some of your plants and the weather is never going to behave. But do not let that get to you. Instead, just head outside and enjoy being a part of your small patch of nature.

I like to set aside a small amount of time each day and dedicate this to the garden. It could be as short as ten minutes, but for me it is vital I get outside to the garden, or the allotment at least once a day. During the summer months this allotted time is when I water my plants. Being surrounded by the peace and tranquillity of new life, which I helped to bring into the world, brings me so much joy, even on the worst days. It allows me to rest my mind and escape reality for a few valuable moments.

I have put together for you a small list of jobs I find really help relax my mind.

MY TOP TEN GARDEN ACTIVITIES TO RELAX THE MIND:

1. Watering with a watering can and inspecting your plants.

2. Rake up fallen leaves into a pile (sometimes I love to kick the pile or even dive onto it and start again).

3. Sow fast-growing vegetable seeds such as radishes.

4. Sow some vibrant easy to grow flowers such as sunflowers.

5. Install a bird feeder, be responsible for keeping it topped up and sit to watch them from time to time.

6. Plant some pollinators' favourite flowers such as foxgloves and buddleia, and watch the butterflies and bees collect pollen.

7. Remove the dead heads off your flowers.

8. Sit under the shade of a tree on a sunny day with a cold drink and enjoy the sounds and smells.

9. Cook a delicious meal on an outside grill or firepit.

10. Give any outside furniture a spring clean using warm water.

The social side of gardening

Today, thanks to our phones and software such as Skype or Zoom, we are more connected than we have ever been. But has this come at a cost? More and more people are remote working, or working from home, and this combined with a rise in the number of people living alone, means social isolation is becoming a growing problem, not just for the older generations but younger ones too. I know all too well how damaging this can be. I went from a busy work environment, packed full of amazing characters of all ages, to being alone in a small office in my house. Almost immediately I felt a change in my mood, the sense of isolation struck within the first two weeks.

Being alone can enhance any stress or anxiety you may have, as you have no outlet to express your feelings, whether that is failures or successes. Luckily there are so many ways your garden and gardening in general can be used as step towards meeting new people, engaging with your local community and building meaningful relationships.

Gardeners on the whole are a social bunch; head to any open garden or allotment and most people working away will greet you or even stop to have a chat. What is fascinating is how in a garden or gardening environment, different generations can and do interact and form friendships in a way that would be rare elsewhere. Some of my best friendships have been with people from different generations, and they all started with a common love of gardening and being out-doors. The great part is, as you shall see, you do not even need a large garden or a garden at all for that matter, to benefit from the social side of gardening.

So just how might our gardens and gardening help to cure potential loneliness?

Build relationships

I am sure we have all seen the old pictures from the 1940s and 50s, where neighbours were stood having a chat over the garden fence while their children played outside in the garden. Over the years the fences seem to have got taller, and the children have retreated inside the house. Unless you happen to catch your neighbour walking from their car to the front door, often many of us hardly speak. Spending time outside in the garden gives you a better chance of interacting with your neighbours, which in my case evolved into barbecues and other social gatherings. Also, if you are growing food in your garden, chances are you may have an abundance in the late summer months, and giving a basket of fresh produce to your neighbours is a great way to start building a relationship.

That relationship does not have to be an in-person one either these days, thanks to social media! When used for good, social media is an amazing tool, and it is fabulous at bringing people together. Across my Joe's Garden platforms, we have well over two million followers from all over the globe. The sense of community has really surprised me over the last three years. There is not just a connection between myself and my followers, but also between the followers themselves. I love to see conversations in the comment sections where people help one another, and what is fantastic is these conversations are often between people whose paths would never cross in real life!

While I am lucky to have a very large following, I remember the days when I had a few hundred followers. This small community was amazing, as back then it was far easier to reply to and engage with everyone, and I almost felt as if we all knew each other. It might not be for everyone, as it can be quite daunting, but sharing your gardening journey on social media is a brilliant way to connect with other people across the globe.

GARDEN OR HORTICULTURE CLUBS

In most areas you will have local gardening or horticulture clubs, which you can usually join for a very small fee These clubs often hold events such as plant sales, seed swaps and plant shows, which are all great ways to become a part of a small but very friendly community. My local garden club holds a tea and cake reception every Wednesday, where you can just go and have a chat. At the last cake reception I visited, the youngest person was eighteen and the oldest was nine-ty-seven, all sharing stories and having a great time!

JOIN YOUR LOCAL ALLOTMENT OR SHARED GARDEN

If you are lucky enough to live in a country that offers allotments or shared gardens, I highly recommend putting your name on the wait-ing list. Allotments are the most social outside spaces I can think of. Most allotments will have sharing tables, seed swaps, summer events, harvest swaps and sometimes even little festivals. On top of that, due to allotment plots being so close together, it is inevitable you will develop friendships with your neighbouring plot holders. It is just an amazing, friendly and cheap way to enjoy all the benefits your garden and gardening can offer.

COMMUNITY VOLUNTEERING

Local councils are often looking for a team of volunteers to help with certain garden or green space projects. Last year I volunteered to help plant out bedding plants in the flower borders near where I live and it was a blast. I still keep in touch with some of the people I met on that day.

THE GARDEN AS A SOCIAL SPACE

Two years ago, I built a small patio area in my garden, with a fire pit and barbecue. This was probably the best addition I have made. Since then, we have hosted countless barbecues with friends and family, toasted marshmallows around the fire pit with the neighbours and even set up a small open-air cinema screen in the summer, for friends to come over and enjoy the big sporting events with us. The garden has now evolved from this very private space to a great hosting area, which the fire pit allows us to use pretty much year-round.

FOOD DONATIONS

Even the smallest vegetable patch can produce excess in the late summer months. I have a relatively small vegetable patch and with a bit of planning, during the summer months it often provides enough fresh vegetables for all the family, some friends, plus a few donations to the local food bank. Not only does dropping off fresh food for others to enjoy make you feel good and give you a real sense of accomplishment, it also helps you to socialize within your local community!

Building your wellbeing garden

Now we have established a few ways your garden can help with your mental health, let's have some fun and think about designing our wellbeing garden, or where we might be able to make small changes to improve our current garden. Obviously building your wellbeing garden is a highly personal experience, as it will be your space, tailored for your needs. However, I would like to offer a simple framework of what I consider when I build my own gardens, and hopefully you may pick up an idea or two you would like to carry across to your own.

The most important part to remember is to have fun, express yourself and enjoy the process. It is so easy these days to compare yourself to others. Ignore those gardens you might see online or on TV, and just focus on what you are doing. Yes, by all means use them for inspiration but try to avoid comparison or competition. As someone whose garden has featured on TV, I can promise you they carefully select the best parts and leave out the rest. My lovely blooming flower borders made the final edit, whereas my giant overgrown section of weeds, dead plants and steaming DIY compost heap did not.

Where to start?

For me, all my ideas start off by sitting down with a pen and some paper, and garden design is no different. Often a garden will be a space shared with friends, family or neighbours, and if that is the case, it would be wise to bring them on board with the planning of the garden. By sitting down together, you can establish what elements your garden will need from the outset.

I like to consider five key factors when thinking about any wellbeing garden design, and these are:

1. The available space in the garden. Are you converting a small balcony or a sprawling, large plot of land?

2. Will your design have an impact on your neighbours or the surrounding community?

3. Is the garden satisfying all of your senses, while also being cautious of sensory overload?

4. What are the goals of the garden?

5. How much will the garden build cost? Gardens can be built relatively inexpensively, but that may require some creativity.

SPACE

The amount of available space is arguably the most important factor to consider before you dive head first into planning everything you want your garden to include. It is wise to start off by mapping out the available space, what can be put where and anything that can't be easily moved or changed. This is especially important if space is at a premium.

I like to measure my garden with a tape measure and draw it out on some paper, so you can get a rough guide as to what you are working with. This does not have to be a timeless art masterpiece, in fact none of mine are every much more than a few 2D shapes! I go off a guide where 30 cm (1 foot) of length in the garden would be 2.5 cm (1 in) on paper, so I can roughly recreate a scaled-down garden. Ponds are drawn as crude circles, sheds are a square and paths are just shaded lines. Once you have mapped out the space in your garden, this is where the fun begins, as you can start to think about all the exciting projects you can fill this space with. If you are a computer whizz, you can really bring your garden to life on a screen too!

We all have different-sized gardens and different goals for those gardens. If you are working with very limited space, it is a good idea to list everything you want your garden to contain and then pick your top few from this list. It is very easy to fill up a small space and less is often more. However, as I mentioned, this is your space and it has to fit your needs, so go wild and fill it up if that's what will make you happy!

The larger the space you have, generally, the easier your garden design will be as you have more options, but by no means does this mean if you only have a small space you should be put off. Even the smallest gardens can bring a lot of joy and achieve so much. You just might have to find a few more creative ways to use that space.

So here are five of my top tips to help utilize small space:

1. Try to grow your plants vertically. So many plants, such as strawberries, cucumbers and clematis, will happily grow vertically up a trellis, which will save you valuable floor space. You can also use vertical containers such as grow towers, or modified pallets.

2. Use the correct variety of plants for your space. A vast number of dwarf variety plants are now available, and unless the look you are going for is that of an overgrown jungle, it may be a good idea to use these dwarf varieties.

3. Less can often be more in a small-space garden. Maybe think about prioritizing a few key goals you would like to achieve and try to accomplish those, rather than trying to achieve a little bit of everything.

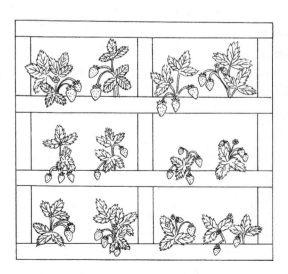

4. If you don't have space for flower borders or vegetable beds, use containers. You can achieve so much with a few small pots dotted around your space and they also come with the added benefit of being transportable, which is especially handy if you are renting.

5. Flexible and foldable furniture is your best friend in a small garden. This allows you to double up the usage of certain areas, as you can fold out or move tables and chairs to create a dining or socializing space, then fold them away once you are finished.

IMPACT ON NEIGHBOURS

Having spent a large part of this chapter talking about how a well-being garden can bring you closer to your neighbours and the local community, a poorly planned garden can be one of the main causes of neighbourhood disputes.

Communication is key, as it can prevent conflict and save any unexpected shocks. A good example of this would be keeping poultry or bees. Both are great additions to the garden but can impact the neighbourhood. It would be a good idea to check if anyone is allergic to bee stings before spending a small fortune on bees and bee keeping equipment. If a neighbour is allergic, this may not necessarily mean you cannot keep bees, it might just mean that person may need to take precautions such as keeping an EpiPen on them, but they will appreciate the warning and it should prevent any issues further down the line. After a few jars of fresh honey or a few fresh eggs have been left on their doorstep, your neighbours should soon accept your new additions.

It is also a good idea to think about where you are going to plant large plants or build structures such as sheds. As a general rule, I avoid planting large plants or building near fences, as plants can soon encroach into your neighbour's property or could cast shade into their garden.

Here are few factors I consider to avoid impacting my neighbour's enjoyment of their property:

1. Will my plant or structure cast shade onto their property? It is inevitable large trees or plants will cast some shade into surrounding gardens, but will planting in certain areas cast shade onto a vegetable patch or seating area, for example?

2. Avoid planting invasive species directly in the soil. Some plants such as bamboo and mint can easily spread throughout the garden and often into surrounding gardens, becoming a nightmare to remove. If you do want to grow an invasive species, consider growing it in pots or large containers.

3. Think about noise levels. Obviously at times gardens can be loud, but it is normally for short periods of time, such as when you mow the lawn. When I mention noise, I am referring to a more permanent background noise such as pumps for ponds or sprinkler systems. A really common device in urban areas are fox/cat alarms, and it goes without saying I strongly discourage the use of these; not only are they not very effective, but they have a tendency to be triggered at all hours.

4. Be cautious about strong odours; over time you might not smell them anymore, but trust me, your neighbours will. A good example could be compost heaps. If you live in close proximity to your neighbours, it might be a good idea to consider an enclosed compost bin, rather than a more traditional open compost heap.

All gardens will provide a sensory experience. However, it is the gardens that put a little drop of thought into how you can stimulate each of the five senses– touch, smell, sound, sight and taste– that will most enhance the relaxation and calming effects we spoke about earlier in this chapter.

Getting the balance right can be crucial in turning a garden from just a lovely space to be, into a powerful wellbeing area. Now this is a highly individualistic area of garden design as everyone's senses are different. Some people may be really sensitive to smells, so for them it is best to avoid very fragrant flowers, where others might be very sensitive to noise. As mentioned earlier, the key part of garden design is to have fun and express yourself. So please do not get too bogged down in making this perfect, over time you can add or remove parts of your garden to find the balance.

These are a few examples of how I stimulate each of my senses in my garden, which you may like to try:

Touch: I love the feeling of walking barefoot across grass, it gives me a sense of being connected to nature while feeling soft underfoot. As a result, an area of well-kept lawn is essential in my garden.

Smell: I strongly associate smells with memories. In a way my garden almost acts as a time machine. Smelling different flowers, especially roses, will often transport me back to happy summer memories. Due to this, I like to be able to distinguish the different fragrances from each plant and avoid having strong aromas that compete with each other. My garden is a mix of heavily scented plants, such as roses and tomatoes, with lightly scented plants, such as sunflowers and poppies.

Sound: Silence for me is a little disconcerting, whereas very soft, gentle sounds have the opposite effect on me. As a wildlife gardener I love the sounds of nature, whether that is birds chirping, insects buzzing or tree leaves rustling, it is all fantastic! I do everything I can to include these sounds into my garden space.

Sight: Bright colours immediately boost my mood, which explains the constant theme of vibrant flowers dotted all over the garden, even into the vegetable patch. Draped across most of the garden I also have solar-powered, soft fairy lights to keep my sense of sight stimulated even in the darkness.

Taste: My favourite part of gardening is growing edible crops. My goal is to be able to walk out into the garden and harvest something to eat on every day of the year. This can be very challenging, but the sense of accomplishment always seems to enhance the taste! If growing fruit and vegetables really is not your thing, you can always utilize edible flowers such as nasturtiums in your flower borders.

What are the goals of the garden?

The beautiful part about building your wellbeing garden is there does not have to be a definitive goal. Often the best gardens have no clear goal, they are just a reflection of the designer's personality and creativity. It is all too easy to get swamped with all the different options, theories and rules of garden design. Upon researching this topic, I found a lot of books and blogs essentially tell you what the goals of your wellbeing garden *should* be. Now to me that is crazy, each individual's wellbeing garden should and will be different. My recommendation would be to not overthink it. Have fun, experiment, let your creativity flow through the space, and then tinker and change as you go. Over time you will discover what works for you and the others enjoying the space.

After all, when building a wellbeing garden, in theory, its only goal is to aid you and your needs. You may set out with a goal of your garden being to provide you with fresh food. So naturally you spend three months designing the best vegetable plot possible for the space available, and then another three months building it. Only then the constant weeding, watering and general attention a vegetable patch needs has the reverse effect and causes you more stress. Whereas, if you keep your garden goals a little bit more open, you might identify what the goals of your wellbeing garden need to be, rather than what you think they are from the offset.

When I build my gardens, I often start with a rough goal in mind. It could be to build a vegetable patch, incorporate a social space or just to add an area to escape reality. Then as I start the build, I learn what areas I enjoy, and focus more on those.

MONEY, MONEY, MONEY!

Money can be the cause of a lot of the health, especially mental health, problems we are trying to alleviate by creating a wellbeing garden. The good news is a garden can be as expensive or as cheap as you would like it to be. I recently took over an abandoned allotment plot, and my goal was to transform it without spending more than £100/$150. In the end I completed my transformation spending only around half of that budget, by just thinking outside the box a little bit and getting creative. Funnily enough, getting creative, plus the addition of knowing I am keeping to a budget, helped improve my wellbeing before the space was even functional. By doing this I picked up quite a few nifty tricks to save money in the garden.

Here are a few money saving tips you might be able to use in your garden:

1. If you have a large space, pallets are your best friend: If you head to most garden centres or builder's yards, they will happily give you free pallets, as they have to pay to have them collected. These can then be broken down for a free supply of wood, to build raised beds, tables, seating areas and so much more!

2. Buy second hand: The rise of platforms such as eBay and Facebook Marketplace, as well as lesser-known sites such as Freecycle and olio, have made finding a deal easier than ever before! I also keep an eye out for car boot sales or garage sales. Last year I picked up an entire greenhouse for free, all I had to do was pick it up, which to save £2,000 was no hardship at all! While that is quite a drastic example, I can often find tools, pots and other bits of gardening equipment too.

3. Plant swaps and seed swaps: Local gardening clubs often host plant swaps or plant sales, where you can find heavily discounted plants and seeds.

4. Out-of-date seeds: Seed packets will have expiry dates, but please do not throw them out once that date has passed. Once a seed gets older the germination rate will often start to fall, but germination rates with modern seeds are so good to start off with, even a reduction is still pretty good! This year nearly all of the seeds I grew were out of opened packets from previous years, and they have grown just fine.

5. Start composting: As primarily a vegetable grower I use a lot of compost. As a result, I am all too aware of the price of compost, and not only has it gone through the roof in price, but in general it has fallen through the floor in quality! The best way to save money here is to start composting at home, even the smallest composting setups will help. For more on composting, see page 93.

For some people a little bit of retail therapy to buy everything they need to have the perfect wellbeing garden is part of their health journey, and to an extent I am the same. While I love to save money where possible, an occasional treat or two can sometimes help as well.

My ideal wellbeing garden list

✳ **Birdfeeders** to help attract an array of beautiful birds, but to also offer a calming background chorus of bird song.

✳ **A hammock** to offer a place to read as well as a space of reflection and comfort.

✳ **A firepit** so you can enjoy your space during colder months and on cooler evenings.

✳ **Water feature/pond** to attract further wildlife into the garden, while offering the relaxing sound of trickling water.

✳ **Solar fairy lights** to give a stunning visual display in the garden, but remember to turn them off once you have finished in the garden as they can interfere with the activities of nocturnal insects and animals such as moths and bats.

✳ **A good barbecue** to encourage you to spend more time in your outside space, while possibly adding to the social element of the garden.

Hay fever / pollen allergy

Across this chapter we have explored a few of the amazing ways we can get outside and use the garden for our benefit, but there is something we need to talk about first, and that is hay fever. Hay fever is essentially an allergic reaction to pollen, and it really is not much fun at all! The easiest way to describe hay fever to those who do not have it is to imagine having a constant cold that lasts throughout most of the late spring and summer months. A few symptoms include sneezing, coughing, sore throat, itchy lips, trouble breathing and sore eyes. Hay fever will prevent you from enjoying your garden and all of its health benefits during the summer months. I am noticing more and more people are suffering from hay fever, and unfortunately, I am one of these people. It is my job to be outside in the garden, so I have picked up few tips and tricks to help manage and limit the effects of hay fever.

My top tips to help beat hay fever:

1. Put Vaseline around your nostrils to trap any pollen before it enters your nose.

2. Wear wraparound sunglasses to protect your eyes.

3. After going outside for a long period of time, shower, wash your hair and change your clothes.

4. Avoid hanging your clothes outside to dry during times when your hay fever is especially bad.

5. Avoid mowing your lawn; grass pollen is often the main pollen to cause hay fever.

6. Wash your pets after they have been outside on a walk as they will be full of pollen. This doesn't need to be every time as you do not want to cause any distress to your pets. I give my little dog a bath every three or four days, but he loves bath time, others might not enjoy it quite as much!

7. Pollen grains descend in the evening as the air cools, so avoid the garden at dusk during times when your hay fever is especially bad.

8. Keep note of the times of the year when your hay fever is at its worst. This will allow you to ascertain with a little bit of research what type of pollen you may be more susceptible to, whether that is grass, tree or blossom pollen. This may help you to then manage it accordingly.

9. The pollen count will always be at its highest during hot dry spells as rain will decrease the quantity of pollen grains in the air.

Good news story

The rise of green social prescribing!

Since the Covid pandemic, the National Health Service in the UK has been heavily investing in the use of green social prescribing.

So, what exactly is green social prescribing? The UK government describes it as follows:

'Green Social Prescribing (GSP) is the practice of supporting people in engaging in nature-based interventions and activities to improve their mental health.'

This is a massive step in the right direction, as gardening and other such activities, are now starting to be recognized, by governments, for the potential healing power they possess.

The UK government are putting nearly £6 million into this scheme, with the aim of focusing on:

* Improving mental health

* Reducing inequalities in health

* Try to reduce pressure on the existing health care system

* Making green social care activities more accessible

While this is still in its early stages, and there is still a long way to go, it is most definitely a gigantic step in the right direction, and I for one cannot wait to see what may happen as a result of this.

Checklist

Have your notebook and pencil handy to make a note of your answers to the following prompts:

→ Head outside into your garden or local open space, and just take five minutes to take in the nature, from animals to plants. Maybe even go one step further and monitor if this has any positive effects on your mood.

→ Is there a specific colour of plant or flower that you particularly enjoy? For me, I cannot get enough of the colour orange, but for many it is the colour green.

→ Have a little think about the different plants and flowers you might be able to plant to bring in a wider range of colours.

→ Spend a few minutes each day exploring a few different outside areas; your garden or balcony is a great starting place, but venture further afield to local parks and woodlands, and make a note if there is a specific area you particularly enjoy.

→ Consider starting your own social media account to track your garden progress and share it with others to build a small community. If you are not comfortable sharing your space with strangers, consider inviting friends, family and neighbours to your own.

→ Next time you are outside, take some time to try
to stimulate all of your senses and pay attention to
whether one might be more sensitive than the rest,
and try to incorporate this into your own garden. For
me, I am receptive to sound so I try to incorporate this
where possible.

Goodbye for now!

And just like that, folks, we have come to the end! I would just like to thank each and every one of you for joining my growing family. I hope you have enjoyed reading this book as much as I enjoyed writing it. Sure, making videos is fun, but there is something special about putting pen to paper, or in this case, finger to keyboard! This process has been thoroughly enjoyable and has given me the prefect chance to reflect on why I am doing what I am doing, and why the garden is so special to me. Without your support, this would not be possible, so thank you very much!

I hope by now you are stood by the door, with your garden shoes on, bursting with excitement to get outside! While we have explored so many ways that we can use our gardens for good in this book, please remember, the most important part is to have fun. Gardening should not be a chore, but rather something to look forward to.

I would like to leave you on this note. Time and time again, I get asked am I worried or concerned about the state of our planet. To that I answer absolutely not, no, not at all! Instead, I am excited beyond measure at this new wave of gardening, which for the most part has a highly eco-conscious approach. Rather than fear, I have optimism and bundles of excitement, and honestly, I think there is good reason why you should too. Positive changes are being made across the globe by many individuals, which I believe will soon give corporations and governments no choice but to stop dragging their heels and follow suit. I am lucky enough to see this on a global scale, every single day, through my social media platforms. Each day on social media countless members of my growing family send me pictures of changes they are making, from rewilding their gardens to upcycling their plastics, and each time I see this, I am reminded that, together, we are making a massive difference.

In fifty years' time when I sit down to write my final book, I am positive the title will be: *How our gardens helped save the world!*

All the best,

Joe

Acknowledgements

It is funny how life works out! If you told me a few years ago I would be sat writing an acknowledgement section of my first book, I would have wanted to believe you, but there is no way I would have. Yet here we are! Getting to this stage has been a tremendous team effort, and I would love to take a little bit of time to thank everyone.

Firstly, a massive thank you to my publisher Pan Macmillan, for giving the opportunity to write this book, and especially to Hockley and her team for helping me bring this book to life! Your passion for the project, and your belief in me has truly helped me more than you could ever possibly realize! I sincerely hope we can work together again in the future.

Another big thank you to my friends and management team at 84 World. Jake, Dan, Chloe, Sophie and Jamie, thank you for always being there and helping me bring my crazy ideas to life! You all work around the clock to help me, and I really do appreciate it.

To my friends at my Hollister in Guildford, thank you for giving me the nickname Farmer Joe, and supporting me during the early days of my social media journey. And to my other friends at home, thank you for putting up with me being absent while I wrote this book!

Without the support of my family this book would not be possible. To Mum and Dad, thank you for letting me steal your garden, for all my crazy ideas! My nan and grandad are the real behind-the-scenes heroes, helping me maintain my garden every day. Without your help this would not be possible. Thank you to my Nonno, for helping to also nurture my passion for all things green, and having an extensive photo collection of baby Joe in the garden. A big thank you to my sister for supporting me in my early social media journey. I love you all!

An extra big thank you to my girlfriend Kamile. Firstly, for helping me in the garden, and for putting up with me when we have to film the videos. But also, for helping me bring my ideas to life with your beautiful illustrations for this book. Without you by my side I would not be able to do any of this, I love and appreciate you so much!

To my growing social media family, I owe this book to you. Without your support for my videos, I would never have found myself in this position, and for that I will forever be grateful. You all inspire and motivate me every day, and thank you for letting me share my garden journey with you all.

Last but not least I would like to thank my great-grandmother Maisy, without whom, who knows if I even would have found the wonderful world of gardening. Thank you for the life lessons you left me with, and I hope you looking down with a big smile!

I have loved every day of research and writing for this book, and I hope it allows you to find as much joy in your garden as mine has brought me over the years!

Thank you all.

Notes

Notes

Index

Note: page numbers in **bold** refer to diagrams, page numbers in *italics* refer to information contained in tables.